VEGETABLES GALORE!

SPECIAL, UNUSUAL, EXCITING,
EXHILARATING, REWARDING
are the words for this helpful,
provocative vegetable cookbook
for the worn and weary cook!

Here are answers to your
constant problem: how to make
vegetables appetizing to your family.
Here are hundreds of unusual recipes
for cooking and using vegetables
in new and elegant ways that
you never dreamed possible.

Myra Waldo, food consultant to
Pan American Airways and one of the
world's most famous modern
cookbook authors, gives you all kinds
of wonderful ideas to brighten your
menus and delight your family with
the help of healthful,
economical, tasty vegetables.

THE COMPLETE BOOK OF
VEGETABLE COOKERY

or
how to cook vegetables so your family and friends will rave about them—and you

BY MYRA WALDO

BANTAM BOOKS • NEW YORK

THE COMPLETE BOOK OF VEGETABLE COOKERY

A Bantam Book / published March 1962

*Bantam Books are published by Bantam Books, Inc. Its trade-mark,
consisting of the words "Bantam Books" and the portrayal of a
bantam, is registered in the United States Patent Office and in other
countries. Marca Registrada. Printed in the United States of America. Bantam Books, Inc., 271 Madison Ave., New York 16, N. Y.*

Contents

~~~~~~

Introduction

~~~~~~~~~~~~~~~~~~~~~~~~~~~~~~~~

The very gentle art of vegetable cookery is, in truth, the acid test for an aspiring cook. Prepare your vegetables with *amour,* with love, or at the very least with *tendresse,* tenderness. Perhaps reverence is the word we seek. Both the French and Chinese cuisines treat vegetables with great reverence, bringing out their delicate flavors with a little butter or oil, a minimum of liquid or steam, rather than drowning them in a deluge of water.

Select the smallest and youngest vegetables you can find, for theirs is the sweetest taste, the crispest texture; certainly overgrown vegetables lose in flavor what they gain in girth. Tired vegetables should be shunned, however tempting the price at which they are offered, for there can be no bargains in stale vegetables. They are a total loss to any good cook. Once a vegetable has passed its prime, the virtue can never be restored. There can be no substitute for quality when it comes to fresh vegetables. Again, avoid very large specimens, no matter how imposing they may appear; the smaller, younger vegetables have better flavor. For example, a tiny young carrot is incomparably better than a foot-long giant, overgrown beyond reason.

Vegetables are stepchildren in the family of cookery. The family group has its particular enthusiasts who praise appetizers and hors d'oeuvres; there are those who plump vigorously for steaming plates of soup in wintertime, or refreshing, chilled plates during the warm months. The fish and shellfish groups have their adherents, some of whom are loud in their praises of the leaping beauties of the fresh-water stream, or the denizens of the ocean deep. Poultry is extremely popular in our country, including not only chicken, but also duck and goose. Beef always had its admirers and still has; lamb and veal, too, are well supported. Salads are a mad cult in the United States, especially in the western states. As to desserts, well, their number has always been, and of course still is, legion. Coffee and tea are strongly supported by those who think a meal is a long wait until their favorite beverage is served.

But vegetables? Who ever talks about vegetable cookery? Potatoes—that's something one eats as a matter of habit. Green vegetables? Other than boiling them, adding a little butter, what can any aspiring chef do with them? A great deal, it is submitted, can be done to make vegetables more appealing and more delicious.

There is only one other country in the world where vegetable cookery reaches a lower point than in the United States. That is in England, where the unhappy custom is to drown any greens in a tremendous pot of boiling water and cook indefinitely until all the taste and flavor are boiled away. We do a little, but not much, better. Alas, vegetable cookery in America is, on the average, poor indeed.

But a bright new day is dawning. Firstly, the distribution of fresh vegetables is improving rapidly, because of refrigerated trucks and airplanes that bring crops to the market in a matter of hours, rather than the weeks formerly required by slow freight. Secondly, frozen vegetables are now being marketed all over the country; these are often of excellent quality, frequently being frozen within an hour or two after being picked. In addition, frozen vegetables are to be had the entire year round, rather than just during the few summer months when the particular vegetable is in season. No longer need the joyous, springlike, garden-fresh taste of green peas be denied us even during December, nor need we wait for next summer to enjoy broccoli, or whatever fresh vegetable appeals to us.

With regard to frozen vegetables, the quality is as good as the reputation of the packer. Avoid unknown, poorly identified brands at all costs; frequently they will disappoint by poor flavor and texture. It is definitely worth spending a few cents more per package in order to be assured of high quality, rather than risk producing a finished vegetable dish with an inferior taste, one not fit to serve. A carton of frozen vegetables is sure to be of top quality when placed on the market by a packer of experience and reputation.

To conclude: carefully prepared vegetables can be served as an inspired, ambrosial separate course in place of a salad. The unexpected or unusual dish is often the most tempting.

MYRA WALDO

Cooking Chart for Vegetables

VEGETABLE	PREPARATION	COOKING METHOD	TIME* *(in minutes)*
Artichokes, French	Cut off 1 inch from top, cut off stem. Remove discolored leaves.	Cook uncovered for first 5 minutes in 1 inch boiling water; then cover.	30-40
Artichokes, Jerusalem	Scrub very carefully; pare lightly. Cook whole or sliced.	Cook covered in 1 inch boiling, salted water.	15 (sliced) 15-35 (whole)
Asparagus	Cut off woody stems, remove scales; wash carefully to remove sand.	Cook uncovered for 5 minutes in small amount boiling, salted water; then cover. Or stand upright in asparagus cooker; or use bottom of double boiler and cover with lid.	15-20
Beans, Green or Wax	Wash carefully; cut off strings and ends. Cook whole, or sliced; may be cut into thin strips.	Cook uncovered in saucepan in small amount boiling water for 5 minutes; then cover.	15-20
Beans, Lima	Remove pods, wash beans.	Cook uncovered in saucepan in small amount boiling water for 5 minutes; then cover.	20-30

* It is only possible to specify approximate cooking times, because vegetables vary considerably in size and age.

VEGETABLE	PREPARATION	COOKING METHOD	TIME *(in minutes)*
Beets	Cut off root end. Young beets may be merely scrubbed; older beets should be pared. Cook older beets whole or sliced; young beets should not be sliced.	Cook covered in very small amount boiling, salted water.	30-40 (young) 60-90 (old)
Broccoli	Cut off tough parts of stalk and outer leaves. If large, cut broccoli lengthwise.	Cook uncovered in saucepan in 1 inch boiling, salted water for 5 minutes; then cover.	12-18
Brussels Sprouts	Remove discolored leaves; avoid very large sprouts. Cook whole.	Cook uncovered in small quantity of boiling, salted water for 5 minutes; then cover.	10-20
Cabbage, Green	Remove any wilted outside leaves. Wash carefully. Cook small heads whole; larger heads quartered or shredded.	Cook covered in very small amount of boiling, salted water in deep saucepan.	6-8 (young) 10-15 (old)
Cabbage, Red	Prepare the same as green cabbage.	Cook as above. If desired, add 1 tablespoon vinegar or lemon juice to keep color.	10-20
Carrots	Cut off tops; pare lightly and scrub thoroughly. Cook whole or in thin slices.	Cook covered in saucepan in very small amount boiling, salted water.	20-40 (whole) 12-25 (sliced) 7-10 (very young)
Cauliflower	Remove outer leaves, cut off stalk. Wash well. Use whole or separate into flowerets.	Cook uncovered in deep saucepan in very small amount of boiling, salted water. Add slice of bread to help cut down odor.	20-30 (whole) 8-12 (flowerets)

VEGETABLE	PREPARATION	COOKING METHOD	TIME *(in minutes)*
Celeriac (Celery root)	Cut away leaves; trim. Wash. Pare. May be cooked whole, sliced or diced.	Cook covered in very small amount boiling, salted water.	40-50 (whole) 20-30 (sliced or diced)
Celery	Cut away leaves and trim root. Cut into half, or quarters. Wash well.	Cook covered in saucepan in small quantity boiling, salted water.	10-15
Chard	See Spinach		
Corn	Remove husks and silk only immediately before using; wash. Cook whole, or cut corn off cob.	Cook in plenty of boiling, unsalted water. Add 1 tablespoon sugar to water.	5-10 (cob) 4-6 (off the cob)
Cucumbers	Use only firm cucumbers. Cut off ends, pare lightly. Cut away some center seeds. Cut into quarters or thick slices.	Cook uncovered in small quantity boiling, salted water.	15
Dandelions	See Spinach		
Eggplant	Wash, then pare. Wash again. Cut into slices.	Cook covered in small amount boiling, salted water.	10-15
Kale	Remove veins, wash leaves very carefully in many changes of water.	Cook covered in ½ inch boiling, salted water.	3-5
Kohlrabi (Turnip cabbage)	Cut away stem. Wash, pare thinly. Cook young kohlrabi whole; otherwise sliced.	Cook covered in very small amount boiling, salted water.	25-35
Leeks	Cut away green tops so that only 2 inches of green remains. Wash carefully.	Cook covered in very small amount boiling, salted water.	15-22

VEGETABLE	PREPARATION	COOKING METHOD	TIME (in minutes)
Mushrooms	Wash mushrooms carefully. Not necessary to peel small, young mushrooms. Stems may be sliced, if very firm.	Fry slowly in butter or margarine in uncovered skillet.	8-12
Okra	Wash; slice. To cook whole, cut off stems and tips.	Cook slowly, covered, in saucepan in 1 inch boiling, salted water.	8-12
Onions	Peel off skin lightly under running water. Cook whole or sliced.	Cook uncovered in boiling, salted water. Or fry slowly in skillet with butter or margarine.	10 (sliced) 30 (large) 25 (small)
Parsnips	Wash; cut a slice from top and bottom. Slice horizontally or vertically. Remove core, if tough.	Cook covered in saucepan in very small amount boiling, salted water.	10-15
Peas, Green	Shell only immediately before use. Wash.	Cook covered in saucepan in very small amount boiling, salted water. Add 1 teaspoon sugar, if desired.	8-20
Potatoes, White	Wash and pare. Or to cook whole, scrub with brush, remove eyes. May be quartered or sliced.	Cook uncovered in boiling, salted water. Fry in butter or margarine in skillet. Or bake in oven.	30-40 (whole) 20-25 (cut up) 50-60 (baked)
Potatoes, Sweet (or Yams)	Scrub carefully; do not remove skins. If boiled, remove skins after cooking, if desired.	Cook in boiling, salted water uncovered. Or bake in oven.	30-40 (boiled) 40-50 (baked)
Pumpkin	Cut into pieces, pare and wash.	Cook in 1 inch boiling, salted water.	25-40

VEGETABLE	PREPARATION	COOKING METHOD	TIME *(in minutes)*
Spinach (and other greens)	Remove ends and stems; pick over carefully. Wash in several changes of water, lifting greens out completely for each change to remove sand.	Cook covered in saucepan without adding water, if leaves are young and fresh; add small amount salt. If older leaves, cook in ½ inch boiling, salted water. (Note: do not use salted water for chard; add after cooking.)	5-12
Squash			
Acorn	Wash, cut in half, remove center stringy portion.	Bake, cut side up. Add some sugar and butter or margarine.	45-60
Hubbard	Wash, cut into serving pieces. For baking, do not peel. For boiling, remove rind.	Cook covered in very small amount boiling, salted water. Bake in shallow pan in oven; add some salt, pepper and butter or margarine.	25-30 (boiled) 40-50 (baked)
Summer	Wash, peel and cut into chunks. Very young squash need not be peeled.	Cook in covered saucepan in very small amount boiling, salted water.	15-20
Tomatoes	Wash. Skin may easily be removed (if desired) after plunging in boiling water.	Cook in covered saucepan slowly; do not add water. Or may be fried or baked.	10-15 (boiled)
Turnips			
White	Wash, peel and cut into pieces or slices. Young turnips may be cooked whole.	Cook covered in very small amount boiling, salted water.	10-20
Yellow (or Rutabagas)	Wash, peel and cut into small pieces.	Cook in boiling, salted water.	30-45
Zucchini	Wash and cut into pieces; better results if not peeled.	Cook covered in saucepan in small amount boiling, salted water.	10-15

Artichokes à la Grecque

1 package frozen artichoke hearts
12 very small white onions
1 clove garlic, minced
¼ cup olive oil
3 tablespoons lemon juice
½ cup dry white wine
1½ teaspoons salt
¼ teaspoon freshly ground black pepper
¼ cup water

Let the artichokes thaw sufficiently to separate. In a saucepan, combine the other ingredients. Bring to a boil and cook over low heat 25 minutes. Add the artichokes; cook 5 minutes. Taste for seasoning. Pour into a dish (not metal), cool, then refrigerate until needed. The artichokes will keep about 2 weeks. Serves 4-6.

Jerusalem Artichokes in White Wine

1½ pounds Jerusalem artichokes
6 tablespoons butter
½ cup chopped onion
1 clove garlic, minced
¾ cup dry white wine
1 teaspoon salt
⅛ teaspoon white pepper

Scrub the artichokes, pare and dice. Melt the butter in a skillet; sauté the onion and garlic 5 minutes. Add the diced artichokes; sauté until lightly browned. Mix in the wine, salt and pepper. Cover and cook over low heat 15 minutes, or until tender. Serves 4-6.

Marinated Artichokes and Shrimp

1 package frozen artichoke hearts
1 egg yolk
½ cup olive oil
¼ cup vegetable oil
2 tablespoons prepared mustard
¼ cup wine vinegar
4 tablespoons chopped scallions (green onions)
2 tablespoons minced parsley
1½ pounds cooked cleaned shrimp

Cook the artichokes ½ minute less than package directs. Drain well and chill.

Beat the egg yolk in a bowl; add the oils, mustard and vinegar, beating steadily. Mix in the scallions and parsley, and then the shrimp and artichokes. Marinate in the refrigerator 4 hours, basting occasionally. Serves 6.

Eggplant Caviar

1 medium eggplant
¾ cup chopped onion
2 teaspoons salt
¼ teaspoon freshly ground black pepper
¼ cup olive oil
2 tablespoons lemon juice
2 tablespoons chopped parsley

Wash and dry the eggplant. Place on a baking sheet and bake in a 400° oven 45 minutes, or until skin is browned and split. Turn eggplant several times. Peel the eggplant, then chop with the onion until very fine. Season with the salt and pepper; beat in the olive oil. Mix in the lemon juice and parsley. Taste for seasoning. Serve with buttered pumpernickel. Makes about 2½ cups.

Poireau Vinaigrette
(Leeks Vinaigrette)

12 leeks
¾ cup olive or vegetable oil, or a mixture of both
3 tablespoons tarragon wine vinegar
1 teaspoon salt
¼ teaspoon freshly ground black pepper
2 teaspoons French-style mustard
3 tablespoons minced onion
2 tablespoons minced parsley
1 hard-cooked egg, chopped

Trim the roots and most of the green part of the leeks. Cut lengthwise in half to about 2 inches from the root end. Wash carefully to remove all the earth. Tie with thread into a bundle, or wrap a narrow piece of aluminum foil around them. Cook in boiling salted water 10 minutes, or until tender but firm. Drain well; cool, and remove thread or foil.

Beat together the oil, vinegar, salt, pepper and mustard. Stir in the onion, parsley and egg. Pour over the leeks; chill at least 4 hours, or overnight. Serves 6.

Mushroom Pickles

1 quart cider vinegar
1 teaspoon salt
1 lemon, sliced
¼ cup chili sauce
⅓ cup allspice
2 pounds button mushrooms

Combine and bring to a boil the vinegar, salt, lemon, chili sauce and allspice. Add the mushrooms and bring just to a boil. Remove from heat immediately Pack into jars and refrigerate for 24 hours before serving. Keeps 3-4 weeks in refrigerator, or longer if packed in sealed jars.

~~~~~~

French Fried Mushrooms

1½ pounds mushrooms
¼ cup flour
2 cups vegetable oil
Salt
Freshly ground black pepper

Wash and thoroughly dry the mushrooms. Cut in ½-inch slices, stems and all; toss with the flour. Heat the oil to 375°; fry the mushrooms 2 minutes. Drain well; sprinkle with salt and pepper. Serve 4-6; or pierce with cocktail picks to serve as a hot hors d'oeuvre.

Mushrooms in Parmesan Sauce

1 cup chicken broth
¼ cup chili sauce
½ teaspoon salt
⅛ teaspoon powdered ginger
2 tablespoons minced onion
3 tablespoons butter
1½ pounds mushrooms, sliced
¾ cup grated Parmesan cheese

Cook the broth, chili sauce, salt, ginger and onion over low heat for 5 minutes.

Melt the butter in a skillet; sauté the mushrooms 5 minutes. Mix in the hot sauce; cook over low heat 2 minutes, stirring once or twice. Just before serving, blend in the cheese until melted. Serve on toast, in patty shells or on crisp crackers. Serves 4-6.

Mushrooms, Russian Style

4 tablespoons butter
¾ cup minced onion
1½ pounds mushrooms, sliced
1¼ teaspoons salt

¼ teaspoon freshly ground black pepper
2 teaspoons paprika
1 cup sour cream

Melt the butter in a skillet; sauté the onion 5 minutes. Add the mushrooms, salt and pepper; sauté 5 minutes, or until browned and liquid evaporated. Blend in the paprika and sour cream; heat but do not let boil. Delicious on toast as a first course, or as a vegetable. Serves 4-6.

Oignons à la Monégasque
(Onions in Raisin Sauce)

1½ pounds small white onions
4 tablespoons olive oil
1½ cups water
½ cup wine vingar
1½ teaspoons salt
½ teaspoon freshly ground black pepper
2 tablespoons sugar
3 tablespoons tomato paste
¼ teaspoon marjoram
1 bay leaf
½ cup seedless raisins

Buy even-sized onions. Heat the oil in a deep skillet; add the onions, tossing until coated. Mix in the water, vinegar, salt, pepper, sugar, tomato paste, marjoram, bay leaf and raisins. Cover, bring to a boil and cook over low heat 30 minutes, or until tender but firm. Shake the pan frequently. Chill. Serves 8-10.

Red Peppers in Oil, Sicilian Style

6 large red peppers
1 teaspoon salt
1½ cups pitted Italian olives
3 cloves garlic, minced
½ cup olive oil

Bake the peppers in a 425° oven 20 minutes, or until the skin is black; turn occasionally.

Slide off the skins; discard the cores and seeds. Cut the peppers into narrow strips; toss with the salt, then the olives and garlic. Add the oil; let marinate at least 4 hours before serving. Turn mixture occasionally. Serve as an appetizer. In a tightly closed jar, the peppers will keep a few weeks. Serves 10-12.

Provençale Tomatoes

      4 large underripe tomatoes
      2 tablespoons olive oil
      ½ cup chopped onion
      1 clove garlic, minced
      ¼ teaspoon salt
      ¼ teaspoon freshly ground black pepper
      ¼ cup soft bread crumbs
      4 anchovies, minced
      2 tablespoons minced parsley
      2 tablespoons butter

Wash and dry the tomatoes; cut in half crosswise and scoop out the pulp; chop and reserve. Heat the oil in a skillet; sauté the onion 5 minutes. Mix in the tomato pulp, garlic, salt and pepper; cook over low heat 5 minutes. Blend in the bread crumbs, anchovies and parsley. Stuff the tomatoes, arrange in a baking pan and dot with butter. Bake in a 350° oven 30 minutes, or until tender. Serves 4-8.

Raw Vegetables (To be served with dips)

Select a variety of crisp, chilled fresh vegetables such as celery stalks, carrot sticks, cauliflower flowerets, Belgian endive, artichoke leaves, radish roses, green and red pepper sticks, tiny plum tomatoes and small mushrooms. Arrange them attractively around the dip.

Soups

~~~~~~~~~~~~~~~~~~~~~~~~~~~~~~~~~~~

Crème d'Argenteuil
(Cream of Asparagus Soup)

4 tablespoons butter
6 scallions (green onions), sliced
2 tablespoons flour
1 teaspoon salt
⅛ teaspoon white pepper
3 cups chicken broth
2 packages frozen asparagus, thawed
2 cups light cream

Melt the butter in a saucepan; sauté the scallions 5 minutes. Blend in the flour, salt and pepper. Gradually add the broth, stirring steadily to the boiling point. Add the asparagus; cover loosely and cook over low heat 20 minutes. Purée in an electric blender, then strain; or force through a food mill. Return to the saucepan, mix in the cream and heat. Serves 4-6.

Old-Fashioned Bean Soup

2 cups navy beans
Ham or beef bone
1½ cups diced onions
2 cups diced celery
½ cup grated carrots
1 clove garlic, minced
½ cup diced green peppers
3 quarts water

1½ cups diced potatoes
1 tablespoon salt
½ teaspoon freshly ground black pepper
¼ teaspoon thyme
2 tablespoons minced parsley

Wash the beans thoroughly. Cover with water, bring to a boil and let soak 1 hour. Drain.

In a large saucepan, combine the beans, bone, onions, celery, carrots, garlic, peppers and water. Bring to a boil, cover loosely and cook over low heat 2½ hours. Add the potatoes, salt, pepper, thyme and parsley. Cook 25 minutes. Taste for seasoning. Serves 8-10.

Zuppa de Fagioli
(Tuscan Bean Soup)

2 cups dried white beans
9 cups water
1 onion
¼ cup olive oil
½ cup minced onion
2 cloves garlic, minced
2 teaspoons salt
¼ teaspoon white pepper
2 tablespoons minced parsley

Wash the beans, cover with water and bring to a boil. Remove from the heat and let stand 1 hour. Drain. Add the 9 cups water and the whole onion. Bring to a boil and cook over low heat 2½ hours, or until the beans are tender. Discard the onion. Purée half the beans in an electric blender, or force through a food mill. Return to the soup.

Heat the oil in a skillet; sauté the minced onion 10 minutes. Stir in the garlic for 1 minute. Add to the soup with the salt and pepper. Cook 10 minutes. Stir in the parsley and serve. Serves 6-8.

For *Pasta e Fagioli,* add 1 cup half-cooked small macaroni or spaghetti when adding the sautéed onions.

Potage Crème aux Choux
(Cream of Cabbage Soup)

>   *4 tablespoons butter*
>   *1½ cups sliced potatoes*
>   *4 cups shredded cabbage*
>   *¾ cup sliced onions*
>   *6 cups chicken broth*
>   *1¼ teaspoons salt*
>   *½ teaspoon white pepper*
>   *1 cup heavy cream*
>   *Paprika*

Melt the butter in a saucepan. Add the potatoes, cabbage and onions. Cover and cook over low heat 10 minutes, shaking the pan frequently. Add the broth, salt and pepper; cover again and cook 30 minutes. Purée in an electric blender, or force through a sieve. Return to the saucepan; mix in the cream. Heat and taste for seasoning. Serve sprinkled with paprika. Serves 6-8.

Belgian Red Cabbage Soup

>   *4 tablespoons butter*
>   *1½ cups chopped onion*
>   *5 cups shredded red cabbage*
>   *1 pound soup meat*
>   *3 quarts water*
>   *1 tablespoon salt*
>   *½ teaspoon freshly ground black pepper*
>   *1 teaspoon sugar*
>   *1 clove garlic, minced*
>   *1 bay leaf*
>   *1 cup diced tart apples*
>   *2 cups diced potatoes*

Melt the butter in a saucepan; sauté the onion 10 minutes. Add the cabbage; cover and cook over low heat 10 minutes, shaking the pan frequently. Add the meat, water, salt, pepper, sugar, garlic and bay leaf. Bring to a boil, cover and cook over low heat 1½ hours. Add the apples and potatoes; cook 45 minutes longer. Discard the bay leaf and remove the meat. Taste for seasoning. Serves 8-10.

NOTE: Pieces of meat may be served in the soup, if desired.

Sopa Lahana
(Greek Cabbage Soup)

> 1 cup chopped onion
> 3 tablespoons olive oil
> 2 quarts water
> 1 pound tomatoes, peeled and chopped
> 2 pounds cabbage, shredded
> 2 teaspoons salt
> ½ teaspoon freshly ground black pepper
> 2 tablespoons minced parsley

Sauté the onion in the oil 5 minutes. Add the water; bring to a boil. Mix in the tomatoes, cabbage, salt and pepper. Bring to a boil again and cook over low heat 1¼ hours, or until cabbage is tender. Taste for seasoning. Stir in the parsley. Serve with sautéed bread. Serves 8-10.

NOTE: A beef bone may be added to the soup for a richer result, if desired.

Cream of Carrot Soup

> 3 tablespoons butter
> 3 cups sliced carrots
> ¾ teaspoon salt
> ½ teaspoon sugar
> ¼ teaspoon white pepper
> 4 cups chicken broth
> 1 cup light cream
> 1 tablespoon minced parsley
> 1 hard-cooked egg, chopped

Melt the butter in a saucepan; add the carrots, salt, sugar and pepper. Cook over low heat 10 minutes, stirring frequently. Add the broth; cook over low heat 30 minutes. Purée in an electric blender, or force through a sieve. Mix in the cream and taste for seasoning. Serve hot or iced, sprinkled with the parsley and egg. Serves 4-6.

Cold Cucumber Soup

> 3 cucumbers
> 4 cups chicken broth
> 1 cup yogurt
> 2 teaspoons chopped fresh dill, or ½ teaspoon dried
> ⅛ teaspoon freshly ground black pepper

Peel the cucumbers; cut in half lengthwise and cut away the seeds. Dice the cucumbers. Bring the broth to a boil and add the cucumbers; cook over low heat 10 minutes. Purée in an electric blender, or force through a sieve. Cool, then blend in the yogurt, dill and pepper; taste for seasoning. Chill. Serves 6.

Gumbo Filé

> 3 tablespoons olive oil
> 1 cup chopped onion
> 1 clove garlic, minced
> 6 cups chicken broth
> ¼ teaspoon dried ground red peppers
> 1½ cups canned tomatoes
> 1 pound okra, or 1 package frozen
> ½ pound cooked ham, cut julienne
> 1 pound raw shrimp, shelled and deveined, or 1 pound crab meat
> 1 teaspoon thyme
> 1 teaspoon filé powder

Heat the oil in a saucepan; sauté the onion 10 minutes. Add the garlic, broth, red peppers and tomatoes. Bring

to a boil and cook over medium heat 30 minutes. Mix in
the okra, ham, shrimp or crab meat and thyme; cook 10
minutes. Taste for seasoning. Remove from the heat and
mix in the filé powder thoroughly; serve at once. Don't
reheat, as the filé becomes stringy. Serve with rice. Serves
6-8.

Hot Tomato Madrilène

> 4 cups beef broth
> 4 cups tomato juice
> ½ cup sliced onions
> 2 sprigs parsley
> 2 stalks celery
> 1 teaspoon sugar
> ¼ teaspoon freshly ground black pepper
> 2 cloves
> ¼ cup dry sherry
> 8 thin slices lemon
> Paprika

In a saucepan, combine the broth, tomato juice, onions,
parsley, celery, sugar, pepper and cloves. Bring to a boil
and cook over low heat 20 minutes. Strain, return to
saucepan and mix in the sherry. Taste for seasoning.
Heat and serve in bouillon cups with a slice of lemon
sprinkled with paprika in each. Serves 8-10.

Jellied Madrilène

Dissolve 2 envelopes (tablespoons) gelatin in ¼ cup
cold water. Stir into the hot soup until thoroughly mixed.
Chill until set, then serve in chilled cups.

Red Caviar Madrilène

Divide the soup among 8 cups. Stir a heaping teaspoon
of red caviar into each. Chill until set. Serve with a tablespoon of sour cream sprinkled with chopped chives in the
center of each cup.

Minestrone
(Italian Vegetable Soup)

 2 slices salt pork, diced
 4 tablespoons butter
 1 cup chopped onion
 1 cup cooked or canned kidney beans
 1 cup shredded cabbage
 1 package frozen green peas
 1 package frozen lima beans
 1 cup diced potatoes
 8 cups beef broth
 1 clove garlic, minced
 2 teaspoons salt
 ½ teaspoon freshly ground black pepper
 ½ teaspoon oregano
 ½ cup cooked elbow macaroni
 ¼ cup grated Parmesan cheese

 Brown the salt pork in a kettle; pour off the fat. Add the butter and onion; sauté 5 minutes. Add the kidney beans and cabbage; cover and cook over low heat 10 minutes, shaking the kettle frequently. Add the peas, lima beans, potatoes, broth, garlic, salt, pepper and oregano. Cover and cook over low heat 45 minutes. Mix in the macaroni and cheese. Serve with additional grated cheese. Serves 8-10.

Minestrone Genovese

 2 cups dried white beans
 4 dried mushrooms
 6 tablespoons olive oil
 ½ cup chopped onion
 4 cups diced eggplant
 4 cups shredded cabbage
 2 cups sliced zucchini
 2 cups peeled diced tomatoes, or 2 cups canned
 2½ quarts boiling water

½ cup vermicelli
2 cups salt
½ teaspoon freshly grated black pepper
¼ cup minced parsley
½ teaspoon basil
2 cloves garlic, minced
⅓ cup pine nuts or sliced blanched almonds
⅓ cup grated Parmesan cheese

Wash the beans, cover them with water and bring to a
boil, then let soak 1 hour. Drain. Cover with fresh water,
bring to a boil and cook 1½ hours. Drain. Wash the
mushrooms, cover with warm water and let soak 10 minutes. Drain and slice.

Heat 3 tablespoons oil in a saucepan; sauté the onion
5 minutes. Stir in the mushrooms, eggplant, cabbage and
zucchini until coated with the oil. Add tomatoes, water
and beans. Bring to a boil and cook over low heat 30
minutes. Mix in the vermicelli, salt and pepper; cook 10
minutes, or until vermicelli is tender.

In an electric blender combine parsley, basil, garlic,
nuts, cheese and remaining oil. Turn motor on until
paste is formed. Or pound ingredients to a paste, gradually adding oil. Stir into the soup. Serves 8-10.

Cream of Mushroom Soup

1 pound mushrooms
3 tablespoons butter
2 tablespoons minced onion
2 tablespoons flour
6 cups chicken broth
¼ teaspoon white pepper
¾ cup heavy cream

Wash and drain the mushrooms. Chop the stems and
half the caps. Slice the remaining caps thin. Melt the
butter in a saucepan; sauté the chopped mushrooms and
onion 5 minutes. Blend in the flour; add the broth, stirring steadily to the boiling point. Add the sliced mushrooms and pepper; cook over low heat 15 minutes. Mix

in the cream; taste for seasoning. Serve sprinkled with parsley, if desired. Serves 8-10.

Mushroom-Noodle Soup

Add 1½ cups cooked, drained fine noodles to the mushroom soup. Heat, taste for seasoning and serve. Serves 8-10.

Mushroom-Barley Soup

> 8 dried mushrooms
> 2 tablespoons butter
> ¾ cup chopped onion
> 4 cups chicken broth
> 3 tablespoons fine barley
> 1 small bay leaf
> 2 sprigs parsley
> ¼ teaspoon freshly ground black pepper
> 1 tablespoon flour
> 1 cup milk

Wash the mushrooms; cover with lukewarm water and soak 15 minutes, or until soft enough to cut. Drain, reserving the liquid. Cut in julienne pieces.

Melt the butter in a saucepan; sauté the onion 10 minutes, stirring frequently. Add the broth and bring to a boil. Add the mushrooms, barley, bay leaf, parsley and pepper. Cook over low heat 45 minutes, or until barley is tender. Discard the bay leaf and parsley. Mix the flour and milk until smooth. Stir into the soup until boiling. Cook 5 minutes longer. Taste for seasoning. Serves 4-6.

Onion Soup

> 4 tablespoons butter
> 5 cups thinly sliced onions
> 6 cups beef broth
> 1 cup dry white wine
> 8 slices French bread, toasted
> 1 cup grated Gruyère or Swiss cheese

Melt the butter in a saucepan, sauté the onions 20 minutes, stirring frequently. Add the broth and wine; cook over low heat 20 minutes. Taste for seasoning. Pour into 8 heatproof bowls. Place a slice of toast in each and sprinkle with the cheese. Place in a 450° oven about 5 minutes, until cheese melts. Serves 8.

Soupe à l'Oignon à la Crème
(Creamed Onion Soup)

4 tablespoons butter
4 cups thinly sliced onions
1 tablespoon flour
1½ quarts water
2 teaspoons salt
¼ teaspoon white pepper
2 egg yolks
1 cup heavy cream
Grated Gruyère or Parmesan cheese

Melt the butter in a saucepan; sauté the onions over low heat about 20 minutes, until browned. Mix in the flour and sauté another 5 minutes. Add the water, salt and pepper. Cover loosely and cook over low heat 25 minutes.

Beat the egg yolks and cream in a bowl. Gradually add about 3 cups of the soup, stirring steadily to prevent curdling. Return to balance of soup. Heat, mixing steadily, but do not let boil. Serve with a bowl of grated cheese. Serves 6-8.

Rumanian Onion Soup

4 tablespoons butter
4 cups sliced onions
1 cup sliced potatoes
6 cups beef broth
1 cup dry white wine

3 tablespoons lemon juice
1 tablespoon sugar
¼ teaspoon freshly ground black pepper
1 cup heavy cream

Melt the butter in a saucepan; lightly brown the onions in it. Add the potatoes and broth. Cover, bring to a boil and cook over low heat 30 minutes. Purée in an electric blender or force through a sieve.

Return to saucepan; mix in the wine, lemon juice, sugar and pepper. Bring to a boil and cook over low heat 15 minutes. Stir in the cream, heat and taste for seasoning. Serves 8-10.

Cream of Green Pea Soup

5 cups water
2 pounds peas, shelled, or 2 packages frozen, thawed
¼ cup chopped onion
1¼ teaspoons salt
¼ teaspoon white pepper
1 teaspoon sugar
2 tablespoons flour
2 cups light cream
⅛ teaspoon nutmeg

Bring the water to a boil; add the peas, onion, salt, pepper and sugar. Bring to a boil, cover and cook over low heat 20 minutes. Purée in an electric blender, or force through a sieve. Return to the saucepan. Mix the flour, cream and nutmeg until smooth. Add to the soup, stirring steadily to the boiling point. Cook over low heat 5 minutes longer. Taste for seasoning. Serves 6-8.

Iced Pea Soup

1 pound peas, shelled, or 1 package frozen, thawed
¼ cup sliced onions
1 cup water

1 teaspoon salt
¼ teaspoon white pepper
1 tablespoon potato flour or cornstarch
4 cups chicken broth
¾ cup light cream
2 teaspoons minced fresh mint (optional)

Combine the peas, onions, water, salt and pepper in a saucepan. Bring to a boil and cook over low heat 15 minutes. Purée in an electric blender, or force through a sieve. Return to the saucepan and blend in the potato flour. Gradually add the broth, stirring steadily to the boiling point. Cook over low heat 5 minutes longer. Chill, stirring occasionally. Mix in the cream. Taste for seasoning. Serve sprinkled with mint, if desired. Serves 6-8.

Peasant Soup

3 tablespoons olive oil
2 cups shredded cabbage
1½ cups thinly sliced carrots
4 leeks, thinly sliced
1 parsnip, thinly sliced
8 cups chicken broth
1 teaspoon salt
¼ teaspoon freshly ground black pepper
1 bay leaf
1 package frozen mixed vegetables
¼ cup raw rice
½ pound spinach, shredded

Heat the oil in a saucepan; mix in the cabbage, carrots, leeks and parsnip; cover and cook over low heat 10 minutes, shaking the pan frequently. Add the broth, salt, pepper and bay leaf. Bring to a boil and cook over medium heat 10 minutes. Add the mixed vegetables and rice; cook 20 minutes. Add the spinach; cook 10 minutes. Taste for seasoning and discard the bay leaf. Serves 8-10.

Potage Santé
(Green Soup)

>   5 tablespoons butter
>   6 leeks, sliced
>   3 cups sliced potatoes
>   6 cups chicken broth
>   1 bunch water cress
>   ½ pound sorrel or spinach
>   1 cup shredded lettuce
>   1 teaspoon salt
>   ¼ teaspoon white pepper
>   1 cup heavy cream

Melt the butter in a saucepan; sauté the leeks 5 minutes. Add the potatoes and broth; cook over medium heat 10 minutes. Mix in the water cress, sorrel, lettuce, salt and pepper; cook over low heat 20 minutes. Purée in an electric blender, or force through a sieve. Return to saucepan; mix in the cream. Heat and taste for seasoning. Serves 6-8.

Cream of Potato Soup

>   1½ cups sliced onions
>   4 tablespoons butter
>   4 cups diced potatoes
>   4 cups chicken broth
>   1 teaspoon salt
>   ⅛ teaspoon white pepper
>   1 bay leaf
>   1 stalk celery
>   1 egg yolk
>   1 cup light cream

Sauté the onions in the butter 5 minutes. Add the potatoes; cover and cook over low heat 5 minutes. Add the broth, salt, pepper, bay leaf and celery. Cover, bring to a boil and cook over low heat 30 minutes. Discard the bay leaf and celery. Purée the vegetables in an electric blender, or force through a sieve.

Beat the egg yolk and cream in a bowl. Gradually add the hot soup, stirring steadily to prevent curdling. Return to the saucepan. Heat, but do not let boil. Taste for seasoning. Serves 6-8.

Cream of Sorrel Soup

> 1½ pounds sorrel (sour grass)
> 1 cup minced scallions (green onions)
> 2 quarts water or chicken broth
> 2 teaspoons salt
> 2 tablespoons sugar
> 1 tablespoon lemon juice
> 3 egg yolks
> 2 cups light cream

Wash the sorrel in several changes of water. Cut off and discard the stems; tear the leaves in half. Combine the sorrel, scallions, water and salt; bring to a boil and cook over low heat 30 minutes. Add the salt, sugar and lemon juice; cook 10 minutes longer. Taste for seasoning. Purée in an electric blender, or force through a sieve.

Beat the egg yolks and cream in a bowl; gradually add the hot soup, stirring steadily to prevent curdling. Chill. Serve with a dab of whipped or sour cream. Serves 8-10.

Cream of Spinach Soup

> 1 pound spinach, or 1 package, frozen
> 3 slices onion
> ½ cup water
> 3 tablespoons butter
> 2 tablespoons flour
> 1¼ teaspoons salt
> ¼ teaspoon pepper
> 3 cups chicken broth
> 1 cup light cream
> ⅛ teaspoon nutmeg

Cook the spinach, onion and water 10 minutes. Purée the mixture in an electric blender, or force through a sieve.

Melt the butter in a saucepan; blend in the flour, salt and pepper. Add the broth gradually, stirring steadily to the boiling point. Blend in the spinach and cook over low heat 10 minutes. Stir in the cream and nutmeg. Serve very hot, with slices of lemon sprinkled with grated hard-cooked egg yolks. Serves 4-6.

Cream of Tomato Soup

> 4 cups canned tomatoes
> 1 fresh tomato, chopped
> 2 cups water
> ¼ cup chopped onion
> 1½ teaspoons salt
> ¼ teaspoon white pepper
> 1 tablespoon lemon juice
> 2 teaspoons sugar
> 2 tablespoons flour
> 1 cup light cream
> 1 tablespoon butter

In a saucepan, combine the canned tomatoes, fresh tomato, water, onion, salt, pepper, lemon juice and sugar. Bring to a boil and cook over low heat 30 minutes. Purée in an electric blender or force through a sieve. Return to the saucepan. Mix the flour with the cream until smooth; stir into the soup, stirring steadily to the boiling point. Add the butter; cook over low heat 5 minutes. Taste for seasoning. Serves 6-8.

Polish Cold Borscht

> 8 beets, peeled and cubed
> 1 cup chopped onion
> 1 teaspoon vinegar
> 1½ teaspoons salt
> 2 teaspoons sugar

~~~~~~

    6 cups water
    1 cup sour cream
    2 cups cooked diced potatoes
    1½ cups diced cucumbers
    2 hard-cooked eggs, grated
    2 tablespoons minced parsley or dill

In a saucepan, combine the beets, onion, vinegar, salt, sugar and water. Bring to a boil and cook over medium heat 45 minutes, or until beets are tender. Cool. Mix the sour cream with a little of the soup until smooth, then combine with all the soup. Stir in the potatoes, cucumbers and eggs. Chill. Serve sprinkled with the parsley or dill. Serves 6-8.

Senegalese Soup

    3 tablespoons butter
    1 cup chopped onion
    2 leeks, chopped
    5 stalks celery, sliced
    1 tablespoon curry powder
    3 tablespoons flour
    6 cups chicken broth
    1 cup heavy cream
    1 cup julienne-cut cooked chicken

Melt the butter in a saucepan; sauté the onion, leeks and celery 15 minutes, stirring frequently. Blend in the curry powder and flour; gradually add the broth, stirring steadily to the boiling point. Cook over low heat 30 minutes. Purée in an electric blender, then strain; or force through a sieve. Cool; stir in the cream. Serve very cold, with the chicken on top. Serves 6-8.

Vegetable-Beef Soup

    4 quarts water
    2 pounds soup meat, cubed
    Veal knuckle or marrow bone

    2 cloves
    2 onions
    1½ cups sliced carrots
    2 stalks celery, sliced
    1 turnip, diced
    6 leeks, sliced
    2 cups shredded cabbage
    1 tablespoon salt
    1 bay leaf
    ½ teaspoon freshly ground black pepper
    1 package frozen mixed vegetables

Bring the water to a boil; add the meat and bone. Cook over low heat 2 hours. Stick the cloves in the onions and add with the carrots, celery, turnip, leeks, cabbage, salt, bay leaf and pepper; cook 30 minutes. Add the mixed vegetables; cook 30 minutes longer. Skim the fat and discard the bone, onions and bay leaf. Serve with toasted French bread and grated Parmesan cheese, if desired. Serves 8-10.

Vegetable Borscht

    3 tablespoons butter
    4 large beets, peeled and sliced
    2 cups sliced carrots
    2 pounds cabbage, shredded
    1 cup chopped onion
    2 quarts water
    2 teaspoons salt
    ¼ teaspoon freshly ground black pepper
    3 tablespoons lemon juice
    2 tablespoons sugar
    2 cups diced potatoes
    1 cup diced tomatoes
    3 tablespoons minced dill
    3 tablespoons minced parsley

Melt the butter in a saucepan; add the beets, carrots, cabbage and onion. Cover and cook over low heat 20

minutes, shaking the pan frequently. Add the water, salt,
pepper, lemon juice and sugar. Cover again and cook 20
minutes. Add the potatoes and tomatoes; cook 25 minutes longer. Taste for seasoning. Stir in the dill and
parsley. Serve with sour cream, if desired. Serves 8-10.

Vegetable-Clam Soup

>1 package frozen mixed vegetables
>1 can (10¾ ounces) chicken broth
>2 cans (7¾ ounces) minced clams
>1 cup light cream
>½ teaspoon freshly ground black pepper
>Paprika

Cook the vegetables as package directs; drain well. In
a saucepan, combine the undiluted chicken broth, clams,
cream and pepper. Bring to a boil and mix in the vegetables. Taste for seasoning. Serve sprinkled with paprika.
Serves 6-8.

Gazpacho
(Iced Spanish Vegetable Soup)

>1½ pounds ripe tomatoes, peeled
>2 cloves garlic
>½ cup diced onions
>1½ cups diced green peppers
>¼ cup olive oil
>¼ cup wine vinegar
>1 tablespoon lemon juice
>1½ cups ice water
>2 teaspoons salt
>½ teaspoon freshly ground black pepper
>1 teaspoon Spanish paprika
>1 cucumber, peeled and diced
>¼ cup chopped onion
>¾ cup croutons

Be sure the tomatoes are quite ripe; peel them. Purée the tomatoes, garlic, diced onions and 1 cup green peppers in an electric blender, or force through a food mill. Gradually add the olive oil, beating all the while, then stir in the vinegar, lemon juice, water, salt, pepper and paprika. Chill 2 hours (not in a metal bowl). Taste for seasoning.

Arrange the remaining green peppers, the cucumber, chopped onion and croutons in small bowls or mounds, and serve with soup. Serves 5-6.

Vichyssoise

    3 tablespoons butter
    6 leeks (white part only), sliced
    1 cup chopped onion
    2 cups diced potatoes
    2 stalks celery
    3 sprigs parsley
    6 cups chicken broth
    ¼ teaspoon white pepper
    1 teaspoon Worcestershire sauce
    2 cups light cream
    2 tablespoons minced chives

Melt the butter in a saucepan; cook the leeks and onion in it over low heat 15 minutes, but do not let brown. Add the potatoes, celery, parsley and broth. Bring to a boil and cook over low heat 30 minutes. Discard celery and parsley. Purée the soup in an electric blender, or force through a sieve. Mix in the pepper, Worcestershire sauce and cream. Taste for seasoning. Chill. Serve very cold, sprinkled with the chives. Serves 8-10.

*   *   *

Vichyssoise was first made by Louis Diat, a renowned French chef. During World War II he discarded the original name and called it gaulloise, in recognition of General De Gaulle.

~~~~~~~~~~~~~~~~~~~~~~~~~~~~~~~~~~

Fassolia Me Arni
(Greek Bean-Lamb Casserole)

> 2 cups dried white beans
> 2 tablespoons olive oil
> 1½ cups chopped onion
> 2 pounds boneless lamb, cubed
> 1½ cups boiling water
> 2 teaspoons salt
> ½ teaspoon freshly ground black pepper
> 1 bay leaf
> 1½ cups peeled chopped tomatoes
> 2 cloves garlic, minced
> 2 tablespoons minced parsley

Wash the beans, cover with water, and bring to a boil. Cook 5 minutes, remove from the heat and let stand 1 hour. Drain. Add fresh water to cover, bring to a boil and cook over low heat 1½ hours. Drain.

Heat the oil in a casserole; brown the onion in it. Add the lamb and brown. Add the beans, the 1½ cups boiling water, the salt, pepper and bay leaf. Cover and cook over low heat 1 hour. Add the tomatoes and garlic; cover again and cook 1 hour longer, or until beans and lamb are tender. Sprinkle with the parsley. Serves 6-8.

Lima Bean Casserole

> 8 slices bacon
> 3 tomatoes, sliced
> 1½ cups chopped onion

> 4 tablespoons chopped parsley
> ½ teaspoon basil
> 1½ teaspoons salt
> ½ teaspoon freshly ground black pepper
> 4 pounds lima beans, shelled, or 2 packages frozen,
>   thawed

Arrange 6 slices of bacon on the bottom of a casserole. Cover with some tomato slices sprinkled with some onion, parsley, basil, salt and pepper. Spread half the beans over it and repeat the layers. Cover all with the remaining tomatoes and the remaining bacon. Cover the casserole; bake in a 325° oven 45 minutes, or until the beans are tender. Remove cover and bake 10 minutes longer. Serves 6-8.

Lima Bean and Onion Casserole

> 4 tablespoons butter
> 18 small white onions
> 1 tablespoon flour
> 1 teaspoon salt
> ⅛ teaspoon pepper
> ⅛ teaspoon thyme
> 1 cup chicken broth
> 1 bay leaf
> 2 pounds lima beans, shelled, or 2 packages frozen

Melt the butter in a casserole; lightly brown the onions in it. Sprinkle with the flour, salt, pepper and thyme, then add the broth and bay leaf. Cover, bring to a boil, and cook over low heat 15 minutes. Add the beans; cover again and cook 15 minutes longer, or until onions and beans are tender. Shake casserole frequently. Serves 4-6.

Meat and Lima Bean Casserole

> 2 cups dried lima beans
> 6 tablespoons butter or chicken fat
> 3 onions, chopped
> 1 pound boneless lamb, cubed

1 *pound boneless beef, cubed*
1 *2-pound chicken, disjointed*
2 *tomatoes, peeled and chopped*
¼ *cup barley*
3 *cups beef broth*
2 *teaspoons salt*
½ *teaspoon freshly ground black pepper*
2 *teaspoons paprika*
1 *tablespoon flour*
3 *frankfurters, sliced ½ inch thick*

Wash the lima beans thoroughly. Place in a saucepan
with water to cover, bring to a boil; then remove from
heat and let soak for 2 hours. Drain well; add fresh water.
Cover saucepan and cook over low heat 1½ hours. Drain
carefully.

Melt 4 tablespoons butter in a skillet. Sauté onions 10
minutes; remove from skillet. Brown the lamb, beef and
chicken in the fat remaining in the skillet.

Place the beans, onions, browned meats, tomatoes,
barley, stock, salt, pepper, paprika and flour in a 4-quart
casserole; mix gently. Dot with the remaining fat, and
arrange the sliced frankfurters on top. Cover and bake
in a 325° oven 2 hours. Add a little boiling water if
casserole becomes too dry. Correct seasoning. Remove
cover and bake 20 minutes longer. Serve directly from the
casserole. Serves 6-8.

Beet Casserole

1 *teaspoon salt*
½ *teaspoon freshly ground black pepper*
½ *teaspoon celery seed*
1½ *cups bread crumbs*
1½ *cups grated American cheese*
8 *cooked beets, peeled and sliced*

Combine the salt, pepper, celery seed, bread crumbs
and cheese. In a buttered casserole, arrange alternate
layers of beets and the cheese mixture.

Bake in a 375° oven 20 minutes. Serves 4-6.

Choux Gratinés
(Shredded Cabbage in Cheese Sauce)

>   3 pounds cabbage, shredded
>   3 tablespoons butter
>   ¼ cup minced onion
>   3 tablespoons flour
>   1½ teaspoons salt
>   ¼ teaspoon white pepper
>   ⅛ teaspoon nutmeg
>   2 cups milk
>   1¼ cups grated Swiss cheese
>   2 tablespoons dry bread crumbs

Cook the cabbage in boiling water for 8 minutes. Drain well.

Melt the butter in a saucepan; sauté the onion 5 minutes. Blend in the flour, salt, pepper and nutmeg. Add the milk, stirring steadily to the boiling point; cook over low heat 10 minutes. Stir in ¾ cup cheese until melted, then the cabbage.

Turn into a buttered casserole or baking dish, sprinkle with the bread crumbs mixed with the remaining cheese.

Bake in a 375° oven 20 minutes, or until browned. Serves 4-6.

Middle East Vegetable-Egg Casserole

>   1 pound spinach, chopped, or 1 package frozen,
>   thawed
>   2 cups chopped scallions (green onions)
>   1 cup chopped lettuce
>   1 cup chopped parsley
>   1 cup chopped leeks
>   2 tablespoons flour
>   1½ teaspoons salt
>   ¼ teaspoon freshly ground black pepper
>   ½ cup chopped walnuts
>   8 eggs, beaten
>   4 tablespoons butter

Wash the fresh spinach and drain well. Or drain the frozen spinach. Mix together the spinach, scallions, lettuce, parsley, leeks (if not available, use all scallions), flour, salt, pepper and nuts. Mix in the eggs.

Melt the butter in a 2-quart casserole or baking dish. Pour the vegetable mixture into it. Bake in a preheated 325° oven 1 hour, or until top is brown and crisp. Serve hot or cold, with yogurt as a topping. Serves 4-6.

Eggplant Parmigiana

> *1 large eggplant*
> *¼ cup flour*
> *4 tablespoons olive or vegetable oil*
> *¼ cup dry bread crumbs*
> *½ cup grated Parmesan cheese*
> *½ teaspoon salt*
> *¼ teaspoon freshly ground black pepper*
> *½ teaspoon garlic powder*
> *1 cup canned tomato sauce*
> *8 thin slices Mozzarella cheese*

Peel the eggplant and cut into ¼-inch slices. Pour boiling water over them; let soak 5 minutes. Drain and dry. Dip in the flour. Heat 2 tablespoons oil in a skillet; brown the eggplant in it on both sides. Mix together the bread crumbs, Parmesan cheese, salt, pepper and garlic powder. In a shallow baking dish, arrange layers of the eggplant, bread-crumb mixture and tomato sauce, sprinkled with the remaining oil. Arrange the Mozzarella cheese on top. Bake in a 325° oven 25 minutes. Serves 4-6.

Okra and Tomato Casserole

> *1½ pounds okra, or 2 packages frozen okra*
> *5 tomatoes, sliced*
> *3 scallions (green onions), chopped*
> *½ pound Cheddar cheese, diced*
> *¼ pound blue cheese, diced*

Cut the stems and tips from the okra. Place in a saucepan with water to cover, and boil for 2 minutes. Drain well.

In a buttered casserole, arrange alternate layers of tomatoes, okra, scallions, Cheddar and blue cheese. The top layer should be cheese. Cover. Bake in a 350° oven for 30 minutes. Remove cover and bake 10 minutes. Serves 6-8.

Onion Casserole

12 yellow onions (2½ pounds)
1 cup cooked or canned peas
1 cup chopped sautéed green peppers
4 hard-cooked eggs, quartered
1 cup (¼ pound) grated cheese
1 cup white sauce
¼ cup buttered bread crumbs

Peel the onions and cook in boiling salted water 30 minutes. Drain. In a buttered casserole, arrange layers of the onions, peas and green peppers. Arrange the eggs on top. Mix the cheese with the white sauce and pour over all. Sprinkle with the bread crumbs. Bake in a preheated 375° oven 25 minutes, or until browned on top. Serves 6-8.

Peas and Crab Meat

1 package frozen peas
½ pound crab meat
2 tablespoons dry sherry
⅛ teaspoon powdered ginger
4 tablespoons vegetable oil
1 teaspoon salt
1½ tablespoons cornstarch
1 cup bottled clam juice
1 tablespoon cognac

Let the peas thaw for 2 hours. Pick over the crab meat to remove cartilage and shells. Toss the crab meat with the sherry and ginger; let stand 10 minutes.

Heat 2 tablespoons oil in a casserole; sauté the crab meat 3 minutes, then remove from casserole. Heat the remaining oil in the casserole; sauté the peas until separated and heated through. Mix the salt, cornstarch and clam juice together; add to the casserole, stirring steadily to the boiling point. Cook over low heat 3 minutes. Return the crab meat; add the cognac. Heat and serve with rice. Serves 4.

Potato-Cheese Casserole

> 6 medium potatoes (2½ pounds), peeled
> 1 cup cottage cheese
> ¼ cup finely minced onion
> 2 teaspoons salt
> ⅛ teaspoon white pepper
> 1 teaspoon Worcestershire sauce
> ¾ cup milk
> 2 tablespoons chopped parsley
> ¼ cup grated Cheddar cheese

Dice the potatoes; cook in boiling salted water until tender. Drain and turn into a buttered shallow 2-quart casserole. Combine the cottage cheese, onion, salt, pepper, Worcestershire sauce, milk and parsley; pour over potatoes. Sprinkle the grated cheese over the top. Bake in a 400° oven 15 minutes, or until browned. Serves 6-8.

Potato-Sour Cream Casserole

> 3 pounds potatoes
> ½ cup grated Cheddar cheese
> ½ cup dry bread crumbs
> ¾ cup sautéed chopped onion
> 3 eggs
> 1½ cups sour cream
> 1½ teaspoons salt
> Dash of cayenne pepper

Cook the potatoes (in their skins) in boiling salted water until tender but firm. Drain, peel and slice thin. Arrange the potato slices in a buttered 1½-quart casserole. Combine the cheese, bread crumbs and onion; spread over the potatoes. Beat together the eggs, salt and cayenne pepper, and add the sour cream; pour over the top. Bake in a preheated 350° oven 20 minutes, or until browned. Serves 6-8.

Pommes de Terre Crainqueville
(Potato and Tomato Casserole)

>   4 tomatoes, sliced
>   1 cup thinly sliced onions
>   1 clove garlic, minced
>   1½ teaspoons salt
>   ¼ teaspoon freshly ground black pepper
>   2 pounds potatoes, peeled and quartered
>   2 tablespoons butter

Arrange half the tomato slices on the bottom of a buttered casserole. Spread the onions and garlic over them and season with some of the salt and pepper. Place the potatoes in the casserole; sprinkle with the remaining salt and pepper. Cover with the remaining tomatoes; dot with the butter. Cover the casserole; bake in a 300° oven 1¼ hours, or until the potatoes are tender. Serves 6-8.

Potato and Vegetable Casserole

>   1½ pounds potatoes, peeled and sliced thin
>   2 cups chopped tomatoes
>   1½ cups thinly sliced carrots
>   1 cup chopped onion
>   2 cloves garlic, minced
>   ¼ cup chopped parsley
>   1½ teaspoons salt
>   ½ teaspoon freshly ground black pepper
>   1½ cups water
>   ¼ cup olive oil

In a buttered baking dish, spread the potatoes. Mix
together the tomatoes, carrots, onion, garlic, parsley, salt
and pepper; spread over the potatoes. Add the water;
bake in a 375° oven 45 minutes. Pour the oil over the
top; bake 15 minutes longer. Serve hot or cold. Serves 4-6.

Potato and Egg Casserole

> ¼ pound butter
> 3 egg yolks
> 2 cups sour cream
> 1½ teaspoons salt
> ¼ teaspoon white pepper
> 3 eggs whites, beaten stiff
> 2 pounds potatoes, cooked, peeled and sliced
> 4 hard-cooked eggs, sliced
> 3 tablespoons dry bread crumbs

Cream the butter (reserving 2 tablespoons). Beat in the
egg yolks, sour cream, salt and pepper. Fold in the egg
whites, then the potatoes and sliced eggs. Turn into a
buttered casserole; sprinkle with the bread crumbs and
dot with the remaining butter. Bake in a preheated 400°
oven 20 minutes, or until browned. Serves 6-8.

Paprika Potato Casserole

> 4 tablespoons butter
> 2 cups chopped onion
> 2 teaspoons salt
> ½ teaspoon freshly ground black pepper
> 1 tablespoon paprika
> 5 potatoes (2 pounds), thinly sliced
> ½ cup beef broth
> ½ cup heavy cream

Melt the butter in a casserole; sauté the onion 2 minutes. Season with a little of the mixed salt, pepper and
paprika. Arrange layers of potatoes over the onions,

seasoning each layer with the mixed seasoning. Mix the broth and cream, and pour over all. Bake in a 375° oven 1 hour, or until tender and browned. Serves 4-6.

Potato Casserole Mousseline

    5 potatoes (2 pounds)
    ½ cup hot milk
    4 tablespoons butter
    1½ teaspoons salt
    ⅛ teaspoon white pepper
    ½ cup grated Parmesan cheese
    1 cup whipped cream
    2 eggs whites, beaten stiff

Peel and quarter the potatoes; cook in boiling salted water until tender. Drain well and mash smooth. Beat in the milk, butter, salt, pepper and cheese. Fold in the whipped cream and egg whites. Turn into a buttered 1½-quart casserole. Bake in a preheated 400° oven 30 minutes, or until browned and puffed. Serves 6-8.

Sweet Potato and Cranberry Casserole

    1½ cups whole cranberry sauce
    3 tablespoons dry sherry
    ½ cup water
    ¼ cup brown sugar
    ¼ teaspoon nutmeg
    2 tablespoons butter
    6 sweet potatoes, cooked, peeled and sliced

Combine the cranberry sauce, sherry, water, brown sugar and nutmeg in a saucepan. Bring to a boil and cook over low heat 5 minutes. Stir in the butter until melted. Arrange the sweet potatoes in a casserole; pour the sauce over them. Bake in a 350° oven 25 minutes. Serves 6-8.

Baked Spinach and Mushroom Casserole

> 2 pounds spinach, or 2 packages frozen
> 3 tablespoons butter
> 3 tablespoons grated onion
> 1 pound mushrooms, chopped
> 3 tablespoons flour
> 2 teaspoons salt
> ¼ teaspoon white pepper
> ¼ teaspoon nutmeg
> 2 cups light cream
> 4 tablespoons grated Swiss cheese

Wash the fresh spinach, drain well and chop coarsely. Or thaw the frozen spinach and drain well.

Melt the butter in a saucepan; sauté the onion and mushrooms 5 minutes. Blend in the flour, salt, pepper and nutmeg. Add the cream gradually, stirring steadily to the boiling point; cook over low heat 5 minutes.

Arrange successive layers of spinach and sauce in a buttered baking dish, ending with the sauce. Sprinkle with the cheese. Place in a shallow pan of hot water. Bake in a preheated 325° oven 45 minutes. Serves 4-6.

Scalloped Squash Casserole

> 3 pounds yellow (summer) squash
> 3 slices onion
> 1 bay leaf
> ⅛ teaspoon thyme
> 1 cup water
> 2 teaspoons salt
> 4 tablespoons butter
> 3 tablespoons flour
> ⅛ teaspoon white pepper
> 1½ cups light cream
> 3 egg yolks
> ¾ cup grated Swiss cheese
> 3 tablespoons dry bread crumbs

Lightly scrape the squash and slice paper thin. In a saucepan, combine the squash, onion, bay leaf, thyme, water and 1 teaspoon salt. Bring to a boil, cover and cook over low heat 10 minutes. Drain, discarding the onion and bay leaf.

Melt the butter in a saucepan; blend in the flour, pepper and remaining salt. Add the cream gradually, stirring steadily to the boiling point; cook over low heat 5 minutes. Beat the egg yolks in a bowl; gradually add the hot sauce, stirring steadily to prevent curdling. Mix in half the cheese, then the squash. Turn into a buttered baking dish; sprinkle with a mixture of the bread crumbs and remaining cheese. Bake in a 325° oven 30 minutes. Serves 6-8.

Vegetable Goulash

> 2 tablespoons vegetable oil
> ¾ cup thinly sliced onions
> 1 cup diced green peppers
> 1 20-ounce can tomatoes
> 1 cup diced potatoes
> 2 packages frozen mixed vegetables, thawed
> 1¼ teaspoons salt
> ¼ teaspoon pepper
> 1 teaspoon paprika
> 1 teaspoon sugar
> 1 tablespoon cornstarch
> 2 tablespoons water

Heat the oil in a saucepan; sauté the onions 5 minutes. Add the green peppers; sauté 5 minutes. Add the tomatoes, potatoes, mixed vegetables, salt, pepper, paprika and sugar. Bring to a boil and cook over low heat 20 minutes. Mix the cornstarch and water; stir into the vegetables until thickened. Serves 6-8.

Curried Vegetable Casserole

> 1 pound green beans, or 1 package frozen, thawed
> 1 pound green shelled peas, or 1 package frozen, thawed

　　　4 carrots, diced
　　　1½ pounds potatoes, peeled and quartered
　　　4 tablespoons butter
　　　1½ cups thinly sliced onions
　　　½ teaspoon dried mint
　　　½ cup yogurt
　　　2 teaspoons ground cumin
　　　1 clove garlic, minced
　　　¼ teaspoon powdered ginger
　　　2 tablespoons tomato paste
　　　2 cups boiling water
　　　2 teaspoons salt
　　　½ teaspoon freshly ground black pepper

In a bowl, combine the beans, peas, carrots and potatoes. Cover with boiling water. Cover the bowl and let stand 10 minutes, then drain.

Melt the butter in a casserole; sauté the onions 10 minutes. Mix in the mint, yogurt and cumin; cook over low heat 5 minutes. Add the vegetables; cook over low heat 10 minutes, shaking the pan frequently. Add the garlic, ginger, tomato paste, water, salt and pepper. Cover and cook over low heat 15 minutes. Watch carefully and add a little more water if necessary. Serves 8-10.

Ghivetch
(Vegetable and Fish Casserole)

　　　1 cup olive or vegetable oil
　　　1 package frozen green peas and carrots, thawed
　　　1½ cups diced potatoes
　　　1 package frozen French-cut green beans, thawed
　　　2 cups diced eggplant
　　　1 cup shredded cabbage
　　　1½ cups chopped onion
　　　2 cloves garlic, minced
　　　1 cup chopped tomatoes
　　　1 green pepper, cut julienne
　　　½ teaspoon thyme
　　　1 bay leaf, crumbled

3 teaspoons salt
1 teaspoon freshly ground black pepper
6 slices carp, pike, or similar fish

Heat the oil in a casserole until bubbly. Add a mixture of the peas and carrots, potatoes, beans, eggplant, cabbage, onion, garlic, tomatoes, green pepper, thyme, bay leaf, 2 teaspoons salt and ½ teaspoon pepper; mix thoroughly. Cover and bake in a preheated 350° oven 30 minutes.

Season the fish with the remaining salt and pepper; arrange over the vegetables. Bake, uncovered, 35 minutes longer, or until fish flakes easily when tested with a fork. Baste occasionally with the oil in the casserole. Serves 6-8.

Plaki
(Greek Vegetable-Fish Casserole)

1½ cups chopped onion
⅓ cup olive oil
2 cloves garlic, minced
3 cups boiling water
1½ cups sliced celery
3 carrots, sliced
3 potatoes (1½ pounds), peeled and sliced 1 inch thick
1 pound tomatoes, sliced
2½ teaspoons salt
¾ teaspoon pepper
6 slices fish (pike, whiting, salmon, etc.)
3 tablespoons lemon juice
½ cup sliced black olives
3 tablespoons minced parsley

In a casserole, sauté the onion in the oil until browned. Mix in the garlic and water; bring to a boil. Add the celery, carrots, potatoes, tomatoes, 1½ teaspoons salt and ¼ teaspoon pepper. Cook over low heat 15 minutes. Season the fish with the remaining salt and pepper; arrange over the vegetables. Sprinkle with the lemon juice.

Cover and bake in a 350° oven 30 minutes. Remove cover, sprinkle with the olives and parsley; bake 15 minutes longer. Serve directly from the casserole. Serves 6.

Colachi
(Mixed Vegetable Casserole)

3 strips salt pork, diced
1 cup thinly sliced onions
1 clove garlic, minced
1 pound green beans, cut, or 1 package frozen
1½ cups fresh or canned corn kernels
2 small zucchini, sliced
2 tomatoes, chopped
1½ teaspoons salt
¼ teaspoon freshly ground black pepper
½ teaspoon sugar
1 teaspoon lemon juice

Lightly brown the salt pork; pour off most of the fat. Add the onions and garlic; sauté 5 minutes.

In a casserole, combine the onion mixture with the remaining ingredients. Cover and bake in a 350° oven 50 minutes, shaking the casserole frequently, or cook over low heat 45 minutes. Watch carefully and add a little water if necessary. Serves 6-8.

Ratatouille
(Mixed Vegetable Casserole)

¾ cup olive oil
2 cups thinly sliced onions
2 cups thinly sliced green peppers
1 eggplant, peeled and cubed
3 small zucchini, thinly sliced
4 tomatoes, sliced
2 teaspoons salt
½ teaspoon freshly ground black pepper
2 cloves garlic, minced
2 tablespoons minced parsley

Using 2 tablespoons of oil for each vegetable, sauté the onions, green peppers, eggplant and zucchini, each separately in turn, for 5 minutes, and reserve.

In a buttered casserole, arrange successive layers of the vegetables and the tomatoes, seasoning each layer with a mixture of the salt, pepper, garlic and parsley. Sprinkle with the remaining oil. Cover and bake in a 350° oven 50 minutes, removing the cover for the last 10 minutes. Serve hot or cold as a first course or as a vegetable. Serves 6-8.

* * *

The onion, that weeping sob-sister of the vegetable kingdom, is a member of the decorative lily family. Onions have been known to mankind from prehistoric days, although the bulbs of those days were undoubtedly small and were excessively pungent. The onion's place of origin is debatable, although it seems reasonable to assume that it was native to that general region beginning at the Mediterranean Sea with Israel, reaching through Pakistan and into southern India.

Of all the races that have peopled the earth in recorded time, the Egyptians were the most impressed with the onion, regarding it as sacred. It was believed to be a divine food, giving unbounded strength to the eater; Herodotus, an expert beyond reproach, states that the standard food for those who built the great Pyramid of Cheops in Egypt was onions; and further, that the cost of onions for the workmen was the equivalent of two million dollars.

* * *

"This is every cook's opinion,
No savoury dish without an onion,
But lest your kissing should be spoil'd,
Your onions must be thoroughly boiled."
Dean Swift

Vegetables to Serve with Main Courses

~~~~~~~~~~~~~~~~~~~~~~~~~~~~~~

Sautéed Artichoke Hearts

> 1 package frozen artichoke hearts
> ½ cup flour
> 1¼ teaspoons salt
> ¼ teaspoon pepper
> 4 tablespoons vegetable oil

Partially defrost the artichokes. Mix together the flour, salt and pepper. Lightly roll each artichoke in the mixture. Heat the oil in a skillet; sauté the artichokes until browned. Serves 3-4.

Asparagus with Herb Butter

> 1½ pounds asparagus, or 2 packages frozen
> 6 tablespoons butter
> ¼ teaspoon thyme
> ¼ teaspoon paprika
> ½ teaspoon salt
> 2 tablespoons lemon juice

Cook the asparagus until tender; drain well. Cream the butter, then beat in the thyme, paprika and salt, and finally the lemon juice. Spread over the hot asparagus. Serves 4-6.

How to Sprout Your Own Bean Sprouts

Buy dried mung peas in a Japanese, Chinese, Indian or specialty store. Each cup will make about 1 pound of sprouts. Wash the peas, cover with water and let soak overnight. Drain, wrap in a damp kitchen towel and place in a colander. Keep in a dark, warm place 3 days, wetting the towel morning and night with lukewarm water. Toss the peas in the towel to keep them from rooting onto the towel. When sprouted, pick over to remove pea skin.

Braised Bean Sprouts

> *1 pound bean sprouts, or 1 can, drained*
> *4 tablespoons lard or vegetable oil*
> *½ teaspoon salt*
> *½ teaspoon ground ginger*
> *3 scallions (green onions), sliced*
> *1 tablespoon soy sauce*

Wash and drain the fresh bean sprouts. Heat the lard or oil in a skillet; add the fresh or canned sprouts. Cook over low heat 1 minute, stirring constantly. Add the salt and ginger; cover and cook over low heat 5 minutes. Stir frequently, and add a little water if necessary. Mix in the scallions and soy sauce. Cook over low heat 2 minutes, stirring frequently. Serves 3-4.

Tuscan-Style Beans

> *1½ cups dried white beans*
> *2½ teaspoons salt*
> *¾ cup olive oil*
> *2 cups thinly sliced onions*
> *½ teaspoon freshly ground black pepper*
> *2 tablespoons minced parsley*

Wash the beans, removing any imperfect ones. Cover with water, bring to a boil and let soak 1 hour. Drain. Add fresh water to cover and bring to a boil. Cover and cook over low heat 45 minutes. Add half the salt, cover again and cook 45 minutes longer, or until tender. Drain.

Heat the oil in a skillet; sauté the onions until yellow and transparent. Add to the beans with the pepper and remaining salt; toss lightly. Chill. Sprinkle with the parsley. Serve as an hors d'oeuvre. Serves 6-8.

Haricots Verts Lyonnaise
(Sautéed Green Beans with Onions)

1½ pounds green beans, or 2 packages frozen
4 tablespoons butter
¾ cup minced onion
1½ teaspoons salt
⅛ teaspoon white pepper
⅛ teaspoon tarragon vinegar
2 tablespoons minced parsley

Cut the fresh beans in half; cook in boiling salted water until tender but still firm. Drain. Or cook the frozen beans 1 minute less than package directs. Drain.

Melt the butter in a skillet; sauté the onion 10 minutes, but do not let it brown. Mix in the beans, salt and pepper; sauté 5 minutes, stirring frequently. Sprinkle with the vinegar and parsley. Serves 4-6.

Beets with Parsley Butter

8 medium beets, or 2 cans sliced beets
3 tablespoons butter
1 teaspoon salt
⅛ teaspoon freshly ground black pepper
½ teaspoon basil
2 tablespoons chopped parsley

Scrub the fresh beets and cover with water. Bring to a boil and cook over medium heat 30 minutes, or until tender. Drain, and slip off the skins. Slice beets ¼ inch thick. If canned beets are used, heat in the liquid, then drain well.

Melt the butter in a saucepan; add the beets, salt, pepper and basil. Cook over low heat 2 minutes, shaking the pan almost constantly. Sprinkle with the parsley. Serves 4-6.

Broccoli Sauté

1 large bunch broccoli, or 2 packages frozen
1 teaspoon salt
⅓ cup olive oil
2 cloves garlic, split

Wash the fresh broccoli thoroughly; remove the coarse leaves and tough lower stalks. Split stalks in half lengthwise. Place in a skillet with the salt and boiling water to a depth of ½ inch. Bring to a boil and cook 5 minutes. Cover and cook 15 minutes more, or until tender. Drain well. Cook frozen broccoli 1 minute less than package directs.

Heat the oil in the skillet; sauté the garlic until browned, then remove. Add the broccoli; cook over low heat 5 minutes, shaking the pan frequently. Serves 4-6.

Brussels Sprouts with Caraway Seeds

2 pounds Brussels sprouts, or 2 packages frozen
1 cup chicken broth
3 tablespoons butter
¾ teaspoon salt
¼ teaspoon freshly ground black pepper
2 teaspoons caraway seed

Wash the fresh sprouts and trim off the tough outer leaves; cut a crisscross in the stem end of each sprout.

Bring the broth to a boil; add the fresh or frozen sprouts. Cover and cook fresh sprouts 15 minutes, or until tender. Cook frozen sprouts the length of time package directs. Drain well. Add the butter, salt, pepper and caraway seed. Toss lightly until butter melts. Serves 6.

Brussels Sprouts in Brown Butter

> 2 packages frozen Brussels sprouts
> 4 tablespoons butter
> 2 tablespoons lemon juice
> ½ teaspoon salt
> ⅛ teaspoon pepper

Cook the sprouts as package directs; drain. Melt the butter and cook over low heat until browned. Add the lemon juice, salt and pepper; pour over the sprouts. Serves 4-6.

Choux Rouges à la Flamande
(Red Cabbage and Apples)

> 3 tablespoons butter
> 3 pounds red cabbage, finely shredded
> 1½ teaspoons salt
> ¼ teaspoon white pepper
> 3 tablespoons cider vinegar
> 2 cups thinly sliced apples
> 2 tablespoons sugar
> ⅛ teaspoon nutmeg

Melt the butter in a deep skillet; mix in the cabbage, salt, pepper and vinegar. Cover and cook over low heat 30 minutes. Add a little water if necessary to keep from burning. Stir in the apples, sugar and nutmeg; cover again and cook 30 minutes longer, shaking the pan frequently. Serves 4-6.

Boerenkool
(Dutch-Style Cabbage)

> 2 heads Savoy (curly) cabbage
> ¼ pound sliced salt pork
> 1 teaspoon salt
> ¼ teaspoon freshly ground black pepper
> 1 bay leaf
> Boiling water
> 4 potatoes, peeled and quartered

Wash the cabbage thoroughly and cut each head into chunks. Combine in a saucepan with the salt pork, salt, pepper, bay leaf and enough boiling water to barely cover. Cook over low heat 30 minutes. Add the potatoes; cook 25 minutes longer. Drain. Serves 4-6.

NOTE: Spicy sausages may be added at the same time as the potatoes, if desired.

Baked Carrots

> 12 carrots
> 4 tablespoons butter
> ¼ cup minced onion
> 1 teaspoon salt
> 1 teaspoon sugar
> ¼ teaspoon ginger
> ⅓ cup light cream

Scrape the carrots and quarter them lengthwise. Melt 2 tablespoons butter in a baking dish; arrange the carrots in it. Sprinkle with the onion, salt, sugar and ginger, and add the cream. Cover and bake in a 375° oven 30 minutes, or until tender. Remove the cover for the last 5 minutes. Serves 4-6.

Braised Carrots

> 4 cups thinly sliced carrots
> ⅓ cup water

> 3 tablespoons butter
> 1 teaspoon sugar
> 1 teaspoon salt
> 1 tablespoon minced parsley
> ¼ teaspoon freshly ground black pepper

In a skillet, combine the carrots, water, butter, sugar and salt. Cover and cook over low heat 20 minutes, or until tender. Shake the pan frequently. The water should have evaporated and the carrots should be coated with the butter. Sprinkle with the parsley and pepper. Serves 4-6.

Orange-Glazed Carrots

> 12 carrots
> 4 tablespoons butter
> 1½ tablespoons sugar
> ¼ cup orange juice
> 3 whole cloves
> ¼ teaspoon salt
> 2 tablespoons minced parsley

Scrape the carrots and cut in quarters, lengthwise. Cook in boiling salted water 10 minutes, or until tender but firm. Drain.

Combine the butter, sugar, orange juice, cloves and salt in a skillet. Cook until butter melts; discard the cloves. Add the carrots; toss over low heat until carrots are coated. Sprinkle with the parsley. Serves 4-6.

Carrot Tzimmes

> 3 tablespoons fine barley
> 5 cups grated raw carrots
> 1 cup grated apples
> 1¼ teaspoons salt
> 1 tablespoon sugar

½ cup water
5 tablespoons butter
½ teaspoon powdered ginger

Wash the barley, cover with water and bring to a boil.
Let soak 1 hour; drain. Combine with the remaining
ingredients in a saucepan. Cover and cook over low heat
1½ hours, or until barley is tender. Stir frequently, and
add a little water if necessary to keep from burning.
Serves 4-6.

Fried Cauliflower

2 packages frozen cauliflower
¾ cup flour
1 teaspoon salt
2 eggs, beaten
¾ cup dry bread crumbs
Vegetable oil for deep frying

Cook the cauliflower 2 minutes less than package directs. Drain well. Roll in a mixture of the flour and salt,
then in the eggs, and finally the bread crumbs.
Heat the oil to 370°. Fry the cauliflower until browned.
Drain. Serves 4-6.

Cauliflower Polonaise

2 packages frozen cauliflower
6 tablespoons butter
2 hard-cooked eggs, chopped
2 teaspoons minced parsley
2 tablespoons dry bread crumbs

Cook the cauliflower as package directs; drain well.
Melt the butter; stir in the eggs, parsley and bread
crumbs. Spoon over the cauliflower. Serves 4-6.

Braised Celery

> 3 bunches celery
> 3 tablespoons butter
> ¼ cup minced onion
> 1 cup beef broth
> 2 teaspoons Worcestershire sauce
> ¾ teaspoon salt
> ⅛ teaspoon freshly ground black pepper

Cut the bunches in half lengthwise and discard the leaves; cut in 1-inch pieces. (You may leave the bunches in halves or quarters, if you prefer.)

Melt the butter in a skillet; sauté the celery and onion 10 minutes, shaking the pan frequently. Add the broth, Worcestershire sauce, salt and pepper; cover and cook over low heat 25 minutes for the pieces, 35 for the bunches, or until tender but firm. Serves 4-6.

Celery Root in Egg Sauce

> 1½ pounds celery root
> ¼ pound butter
> 1½ teaspoons salt
> ⅛ teaspoon white pepper
> 1 cup water
> 3 egg yolks
> 3 tablespoons lemon juice

Peel the celery root, wash, dry and cut into cubes. Melt the butter in a skillet; brown the cubes in it. Add the salt, pepper and water; bring to a boil, cover and cook over low heat 25 minutes, or until tender. Drain, reserving 2 tablespoons liquid.

Beat the egg yolks until light. Gradually beat in the lemon juice, then the hot liquid, beating constantly. Add to the celery root; cook over low heat 2 minutes, stirring steadily, but do not let boil. Serves 4-6.

French-Fried Celery Root

>   5 celery roots
>   1 quart vegetable oil
>   Salt

Trim and peel the celery roots. Cut into 1½-inch lengths, sliced pencil-thin. Cover with ice water and let stand 30 minutes. Drain and dry.

Heat the oil to 375°; fry the celery root 5 minutes, or until delicately browned. Drain and sprinkle with salt. Serve with a mustard-flavored hollandaise sauce. Serves 4-6.

Celeri à la Moelle
(Braised Celery with Marrow)

>   4 marrow bones
>   3 cups beef broth
>   4 bunches celery
>   4 tablespoons butter
>   ½ teaspoon Worcestershire sauce
>   ⅛ teaspoon pepper

Cook the marrow bones in 2 cups broth for 20 minutes. Scoop out the marrow and cut into slices.

Remove the leaves of the celery and cut into quarters lengthwise. Melt the butter in a skillet; lightly brown the celery in it. Add the remaining broth, Worcestershire and pepper. Cover and cook over low heat 10 minutes. Add the marrow; cook 3 minutes longer. Serves 4-6.

Charcoal Roast Corn

1. Gently pull back the husks of the corn. Remove the silk and replace the husks. Soak in salted cold water 5 minutes. Drain. Place on a grill over hot coals;

roast 10-12 minutes, turning the ears a few times. Pull off the husks.

2. Remove the husks and silk of the corn. Place each ear on a piece of aluminum foil; brush the corn with softened butter. Wrap corn, sealing the edges well. Place on a grill over hot coals. Roast 15-18 minutes, turning them each a few times.

Boiled Corn on the Cob

Buy very fresh corn; to test, prick a kernel with your nail—a milky substance should run out. Remove the husks and silk of the corn. If silk adheres to the corn, use a dry vegetable brush gently to remove it. Have a kettle of boiling water ready: a tablespoon of sugar may be added to each 2 quarts if desired. (Don't salt the water, as it toughens the corn.) Put the corn in the boiling water, cover and cook over high heat 5 to 8 minutes. Lift out with tongs and drain well. Place on a napkin.

Corn Sauté

    4 tablespoons butter
    4 cups fresh or frozen corn kernels
    ½ cup heavy cream
    1 teaspoon salt
    ¼ teaspoon white pepper

Melt the butter in a skillet; stir in the corn for 1 minute. Add the cream; cook over low heat 5 to 7 minutes, stirring very frequently. Add salt and pepper. Serves 6-8.

Breaded Cucumber Slices

    4 long thin cucumbers
    3 tablespoons bread crumbs
    3 tablespoons flour
    ¾ teaspoon salt

    ⅛ teaspoon white pepper
    ¼ teaspoon garlic powder
    ¼ cup salad oil

Wash and dry the unpeeled cucumbers; slice ⅛ inch thick. Mix together the bread crumbs, flour, salt, pepper and garlic powder; dredge the cucumbers with the mixture.

Heat the oil in a skillet; brown the cucumber slices on both sides. Drain on paper towels and serve immediately. Serves 4-6.

Braised Cucumbers

    4 cucumbers
    3 tablespoons butter
    ¼ cup beef broth
    ⅛ teaspoon freshly ground black pepper
    2 teaspoons minced parsley

Peel the cucumbers; cut in half lengthwise, then into thirds crosswise. Scoop out the seeds. Melt the butter in a skillet; sauté the cucumbers 3 minutes. Add the broth and pepper; cover and cook over low heat 5 minutes, or until tender but still crisp. Sprinkle with the parsley. Serves 4-6.

Fried Eggplant Sticks

    1 medium eggplant
    ½ cup pancake mix
    2 tablespoons grated Parmesan cheese
    ¼ teaspoon pepper
    ⅓ cup of cold water
    1 cup vegetable oil

Peel the eggplant; cut in ½-inch slices, then into ½-inch strips. Make a batter of the pancake mix, cheese, pepper and water. Dip the sticks in it. Heat the oil in a skillet until it bubbles; fry the eggplant in it until browned on all sides. Drain on paper towels. Serves 4-6.

Aubergine à la Provençale
(Eggplant Provençale)

>   2 small eggplant
>   2½ teaspoons salt
>   ½ cup flour
>   ⅓ cup olive oil
>   ½ cup chopped onion
>   1 clove garlic, minced
>   1½ cups diced tomatoes
>   ¼ teaspoon freshly ground black pepper
>   2 tablespoons minced parsley

Peel the eggplant and slice ¼ inch thick. Sprinkle with 1½ teaspoons salt and let stand 30 minutes. Drain well and dry; dip it in the flour.

Heat half the oil in a skillet; brown the eggplant on both sides. Remove. Heat the remaining oil in the skillet; sauté the onion 5 minutes. Add the garlic, tomatoes, pepper and remaining salt; cook over low heat 10 minutes, stirring frequently. Return the eggplant and add the parsley; cook over low heat 5 minutes. Serves 4-6.

Aubergines Gratin
(Sautéed Eggplant)

>   1 medium eggplant
>   2½ teaspoons salt
>   4 tablespoons olive oil
>   4 tablespoons minced onion
>   1 clove garlic, minced
>   4 tablespoons dry bread crumbs
>   2 tablespoons minced parsley

Peel the eggplant and slice ½ inch thick. Sprinkle with 2 teaspoons salt and let stand 30 minutes. Drain well and dry. Heat half the oil in a skillet; brown the eggplant slices on both sides. Transfer to a serving dish and keep warm.

Heat the remaining oil in the skillet; sauté the onion

3 minutes. Add the garlic, bread crumbs, parsley and remaining salt; cook over low heat 2 minutes, stirring constantly. Sprinkle over the eggplant. Serves 4-6.

Eggplant, Near East Style

> 4 tablespoons olive oil
> 1 cup chopped onion
> 1 green pepper, cut in strips
> 1 medium eggplant, peeled and cubed
> 1½ teaspoons salt
> ¼ teaspoon freshly ground black pepper
> ¼ teaspoon oregano
> 1 cup chopped tomatoes

Heat 2 tablespoons oil in a deep skillet; sauté the onion 5 minutes. Add the remaining oil, then the green pepper and eggplant; sauté 10 minutes, stirring occasionally. Mix in the salt, pepper, oregano and tomatoes. Cover and cook over low heat 30 minutes. Watch carefully, and add a little boiling water if necessary. Serves 4-6.

Braised Endive

> 6 endive
> 3 tablespoons melted butter
> 2 tablespoons lemon juice
> 1 teaspoon salt
> ¼ teaspoon pepper
> 1 teaspoon sugar
> ½ cup chicken broth

Wash the endive and cut in half lengthwise. Pour 1 tablespoon butter into a shallow baking dish; arrange the endive in it. Sprinkle with the lemon juice, salt, pepper, sugar and remaining butter; add the broth. Cover the dish with a piece of greased aluminum foil. Bake in a 350° oven 40 minutes, removing the foil for the last 5 minutes. Serves 4-6.

Braised Escarole, Italian Style

>   *3 pounds escarole*
>   *⅓ cup olive oil*
>   *2 cloves garlic, split*
>   *1½ teaspoons salt*
>   *¼ teaspoon freshly ground black pepper*
>   *½ teaspoon oregano*

Wash the escarole, discarding the outside leaves. Separate the heads, and cut leaves into pieces; drain well.

Heat the oil in a deep skillet; brown the garlic in it, then discard. Add the escarole, salt, pepper and oregano. Cover and cook over low heat 12 minutes, or until tender. Shake the pan occasionally. Serves 4-6.

Finocchi Siciliana
(Fennel, Sicilian Style)

>   *6 small fennel*
>   *3 tablespoons olive oil*
>   *¼ cup finely chopped onion*
>   *1 clove garlic, minced*
>   *¾ teaspoon salt*
>   *½ teaspoon freshly ground black pepper*
>   *½ cup chicken broth*
>   *4 tablespoons grated Parmesan cheese*

Trim the fennel, discarding the leaves and tough outer portions. Cut into 4, and wash. Drain well.

Heat the oil in a skillet; sauté the onion 5 minutes. Add the garlic and fennel; sauté 10 minutes, shaking the skillet frequently. Add the salt, pepper and broth; cover and cook over low heat 15 minutes, or until tender. Sprinkle with the cheese and place under a hot broiler for 2 minutes to brown the cheese. Serves 6-8.

Kale, Southern Style

> 2 pounds kale
> 2 slices bacon, diced
> ½ cup grated onion
> ⅓ cup water
> 1 bay leaf
> 1¼ teaspoons salt
> ¼ teaspoon freshly ground black pepper

Wash the kale thoroughly; strip the leaves from the tough center ribs.

In a heavy saucepan, lightly brown the bacon. Add the kale, onion, water, bay leaf, salt and pepper. Cover and cook over low heat 15 minutes, or until tender. Watch carefully, and add a little boiling water if necessary to prevent sticking. Serve with lemon wedges. Serves 4.

Braised Leeks

> 24 leeks
> 6 tablespoons butter

Trim the leeks, cutting away the roots and most of the green part. Wash very carefully to remove all the soil. Cook the leeks in boiling salted water 8 minutes; drain well.

Melt the butter in a shallow baking dish. Arrange the leeks in it and baste with the butter. Bake in a 350° oven 15 minutes, or until the leeks begin to turn brown, basting frequently. Serves 4-6.

Lettuce in White Wine

> 2 heads lettuce
> 3 tablespoons olive or vegetable oil
> 1 tomato, peeled and chopped
> 2 cups dry white wine
> 1½ teaspoons salt

    1½ tablespoons lemon juice
    1 teaspoon sugar
    Dash of cayenne pepper

If head lettuce is used, cut into eighths. If leaf lettuce, tear into pieces. Pour boiling water over the lettuce and let stand 10 minutes. Drain and dry.

Heat the oil in a skillet; mix in the tomato and cook over low heat 2 minutes. Add the lettuce; cook 2 minutes, stirring frequently. Mix in the wine, salt, lemon juice, sugar and cayenne pepper. Cook over low heat 3 minutes. Cool before serving. Serves 4-6.

Chinese Braised Lettuce

    2 heads lettuce
    3 tablespoons lard or vegetable oil
    1 clove garlic, minced
    1 teaspoon salt

Wash the lettuce thoroughly. If using Simpson lettuce, shred it. Romaine or leaf lettuce should be torn into 2-inch pieces.

Heat the lard or oil in a skillet; add the garlic. Cook over low heat 1 minute. Mix in the lettuce and salt; cook over low heat 3 minutes, or until tender but crisp. Serves 4-6.

Lima Beans, Southern Style

    2 packages frozen lima beans
    2 tablespoons butter
    ½ cup chopped onion
    ¼ cup chopped green pepper
    1 20-ounce can tomatoes
    1¼ teaspoons salt
    ¼ teaspoon freshly ground black pepper
    ¼ teaspoon basil
    1 bay leaf

Cook the beans 2 minutes less than package directs; drain. Melt the butter in a saucepan; sauté the onion 5 minutes. Add the green pepper, tomatoes, salt, pepper, basil and bay leaf. Bring to a boil and cook over low heat 15 mintues. Add the beans and cook 10 minutes longer. Serves 4-6.

Fèves à la Bourgeoise
(Lima Beans, Family Style)

> 4 tablespoons butter
> 1 cup chopped onion
> ½ teaspoon chervil
> 4 pounds lima beans, shelled, or 2 packages frozen
> 1 cup chicken broth
> 1 teaspoon salt
> 2 tablespoons minced parsley

Melt the butter in a skillet; sauté the onion 5 minutes. Add the chervil, beans, broth and salt. Bring to a boil, cover and cook over low heat 20 minutes (10 minutes for frozen), or until tender. Sprinkle with the parsley. Serves 4-6.

Mushroom Sauce

> 4 tablespoons butter
> ¼ cup minced onion
> ½ pound mushrooms, sliced
> 2 tablespoons flour
> 1½ cups beef broth
> ¼ teaspoon freshly ground black pepper

Melt the butter in a saucepan; sauté the onion and mushrooms 5 minutes. Blend in the flour until browned. Add the broth, stirring constantly to the boiling point. Add the pepper; cook over low heat 10 minutes.
Makes about 2 cups.

Breaded Mushrooms

> 24 large mushroom caps
> ½ cup flour
> 1½ teaspoons salt
> ¼ teaspoon freshly ground black pepper
> 2 eggs, beaten
> ¾ cup dry bread crumbs
> Vegetable oil for deep frying

Wash and dry the mushroom caps. Mix the flour, salt and pepper, then add the eggs and finally the bread crumbs. Dip mushrooms in mixture.

Heat the oil to 375°. Fry the mushrooms 3 minutes, or until browned. Drain. Serve as a vegetable, or on rice as a main course. Tartar sauce may be served with the mushrooms. Serves 4-6.

Mushrooms, Bordeaux Style

> 2 pounds mushrooms
> 2 tablespoons butter
> 2 tablespoons olive oil
> ½ cup chopped shallots or onions
> 1¼ teaspoons salt
> ¼ teaspoon freshly ground black pepper
> 2 tablespoons minced parsley

Remove the stems of the mushrooms and chop; slice the caps. Heat the butter and oil in a skillet; sauté the sliced mushrooms over high heat until browned. Mix in the chopped stems, shallots, salt and pepper; cook over low heat 5 minutes. Taste for seasoning, transfer to a serving dish and sprinkle with the parsley. Serves 6-8.

Spicy Braised Okra

> 2 pounds okra, or 2 packages frozen, thawed
> 4 tablespoons butter
> 3 large onions, peeled and sliced thick

¼ teaspoon dried ground red peppers
2 teaspoons turmeric
1½ teaspoons salt
Lettuce leaves

Wash the fresh okra, remove the stems and dry thoroughly. Or dry the frozen okra.

Melt the butter in a skillet; brown the onions in it. Mix in the okra, red peppers and turmeric; cook over low heat 10 minutes, shaking the pan frequently. Add the salt, and cover the okra with lettuce leaves. Cover the skillet and cook over low heat 10 minutes. Watch carefully to prevent burning. Discard the lettuce. Serves 4-6.

Onions Amandine

1½ pounds small white onions
¼ pound (½ cup) butter
1¼ teaspoons salt
¼ teaspoon freshly ground black pepper
2 tablespoons brown sugar
¼ teaspoon nutmeg
1 cup blanched almonds

Buy even-sized onions. Combine the butter, salt, pepper and brown sugar in a casserole. Cook over low heat until butter and sugar melt. Add the onions, nutmeg, and almonds; shake casserole to coat onions. Cover and bake in a 350° oven, 50 minutes or until tender. Shake casserole frequently and remove cover for last 5 minutes. Serves 6-8.

French-Fried Onions

Cut Spanish or Bermuda onions into slices ¼ inch thick. Separate into rings. Dip in light cream, then into flour. Fry in 375° fat until golden brown. Drain on absorbent paper. Keep warm in a 275° oven until all the onions are fried.

Scalloped Onions and Nuts

> 4 cups sliced onions
> 1 cup water
> 3 tablespoons butter
> 3 tablespoons flour
> 1½ teaspoons salt
> ¼ teaspoon white pepper
> 1 cup light cream
> 1 cup chopped nuts
> ½ cup buttered bread crumbs

Cook the onions in the water 5 minutes, or until tender but still crisp. Drain, reserving ½ cup liquid.

Melt the butter in a saucepan; blend in the flour, salt and pepper. Add the cream and reserved liquid, stirring steadily to the boiling point; cook over low heat 3 minutes. Mix in the onions. Spread ⅓ the mixture on the bottom of a buttered baking dish. Sprinkle with ⅓ the nuts. Repeat the layers, mixing the bread crumbs with the nuts for the top layer. Bake in a 350° oven 20 minutes, or until browned. Serves 4-6.

Glazed Onions

> 24 small white onions
> 2 tablespoons honey
> 2 tablespoons ketchup
> 3 tablespoons butter or margarine
> ¼ cup water
> ⅛ teaspoon salt
> Pinch of cayenne pepper

Peel onions; cook in boiling salted water 20 minutes. Drain; place in baking dish. Heat together the honey, ketchup, butter, water, salt and cayenne. Pour over the onions. Cover and bake in a 350° oven 1 hour, basting frequently. Serves 4-6.

Braised Onions

>24 small white onions
>3 tablespoons butter
>1 cup chicken broth
>¾ teaspoon salt
>1 tablespoon brown sugar
>½ teaspoon Worcestershire sauce

Peel the onions. Melt the butter in a saucepan; sauté the onions 5 minutes, shaking the pan frequently. Add the broth, salt, brown sugar and Worcestershire. Cover and cook over low heat 20 minutes, or until liquid is almost absorbed and onions tender. Serves 4-6.

Glazed Parsnips

>12 parsnips
>4 tablespoons soft butter
>4 tablespoons brown sugar

Scrape the parsnips; cook in boiling salted water 10 minutes. Drain, and cut in half lengthwise. Arrange the parsnips in a buttered pie plate or shallow baking dish. Spread with the butter and sprinkle with the brown sugar. Bake in a preheated 375° oven 25 minutes, or until glazed. Shake the pan occasionally. Serves 4-6.

Black-Eyed Peas, Southern Style

>1½ pounds smoked pork butt
>3 cups boiling water
>2 onions
>4 cloves garlic
>1 teaspoon salt
>½ teaspoon freshly ground black pepper
>1 bay leaf
>2 packages frozen black-eyed peas

Wash the pork butt, cover with water and bring to a boil; cook over medium heat 30 minutes. Drain; add the 3 cups boiling water, the onions, garlic, salt, pepper and bay leaf. Cook over low heat 30 minutes. Add the black-eyed peas. Cook 20 minutes. Drain. Slice the meat and mix with the peas. Serves 4-6.

Indian-Style Chick Peas

>   2 cans chick peas
>   4 tablespoons butter
>   1½ cups chopped onion
>   1½ teaspoons turmeric
>   ¼ teaspoon powdered ginger
>   ¼ teaspoon dried ground red pepper
>   2 tomatoes, chopped
>   1¼ teaspoons salt
>   2 tablespoons minced parsley

Drain the chick peas, reserving ¼ cup liquid. Melt the butter in a skillet; sauté the onion 10 minutes. Mix in the turmeric, ginger, red pepper and chick peas. Cook over low heat 5 minutes. Add the tomatoes, salt and reserved liquid. Cook over low heat 10 minutes. Sprinkle with the parsley. Serves 4-6.

Green Peas Purée

>   1½ cups water
>   1 teaspoon salt
>   ⅛ teaspoon nutmeg
>   ½ teaspoon sugar
>   1 cup shredded lettuce
>   2 pounds green peas, shelled, or 2 packages frozen
>   1 tablespoon minced parsley
>   3 tablespoons heavy cream
>   3 tablespoons butter

Bring the water, salt, nutmeg and sugar to a boil. Add the lettuce, peas and parsley; cook over medium heat 15 minutes, or until peas are tender. Drain well; purée in an electric blender or force through a sieve. Beat in the cream and butter; heat, taste for seasoning and serve. Serves 4-6.

Peas with Bacon

> 4 slices bacon, diced
> ½ cup thinly sliced scallions (green onions)
> 2 tablespoons flour
> ½ teaspoon salt
> ⅛ teaspoon white pepper
> 1½ cups hot beef broth
> 2 pounds green peas, shelled, or 2 packages frozen, thawed

Brown the bacon and scallions in a skillet; pour off all but 1 tablespoon fat. Blend in the flour, salt and pepper. Add the broth gradually, stirring steadily to the boiling point. Add the peas; cover and cook over medium heat 20 minutes for fresh peas; 8 minutes for frozen. Serves 4-6.

Piselli alla Romana
(Peas and Ham)

> 3 tablespoons butter
> ½ cup chopped onion
> 2 tablespoons flour
> 1 teaspoon salt
> ⅛ teaspoon white pepper
> 2 cups chicken broth
> 3 pounds green peas, shelled, or 2 packages frozen, thawed
> ¼ pound cooked ham, shredded (prosciutto, if possible)

Melt the butter in a skillet; sauté the onion 10 minutes. Blend in the flour; add salt and pepper, then gradually add the broth, stirring steadily to the boiling point. Add the peas and ham. Cover and cook over low heat 20 minutes (frozen peas 10 minutes). Serves 6-8.

French-Style Peas

> 3 tablespoons butter
> 1 cup shredded lettuce
> ½ cup thinly sliced scallions (green onions) or onions
> 2 pounds green peas, shelled, or 2 packages frozen, thawed
> ¾ teaspoon salt
> 1 teaspoon sugar
> 2 tablespoons water

Melt the butter in a deep skillet; spread the lettuce on the bottom. Add the scallions, peas, salt, sugar and water. Cover and cook over low heat 30 minutes. Watch carefully and add a little boiling water if necessary. Mix lightly before serving. Serves 4-6.

Sauerkraut, Hungarian Style

> 2 pounds sauerkraut
> 3 tablespoons butter
> 1 cup chopped onions
> 2 cups grated drained potatoes
> 1 teaspoon salt
> ½ teaspoon freshly ground black pepper
> 1 bay leaf
> 2 cloves
> 1 cup sour cream

Buy barrel sauerkraut, if possible. Rinse under cold water and drain well. (If canned sauerkraut is used, rinse it for about 5 minutes.) Melt the butter in a heavy saucepan; sauté the onions 5 minutes. Add the sauerkraut, potatoes, salt, pepper, bay leaf and cloves. Cover and cook over low heat 30 minutes, stirring frequently. Mix in the sour cream; cover again and cook 1 hour longer. Serves 6-8.

Sauerkraut in Champagne

> 2 pounds sauerkraut
> 2 cups puréed apricots
> 4 cups champagne or dry white wine

Buy barrel sauerkraut if possible. Wash under cold running water and drain well. (If canned sauerkraut is used, wash it very thoroughly.) Combine the sauerkraut, apricots (you can use canned baby food) and champagne in a casserole or saucepan. Cover and cook low heat 1½ hours. Shake casserole and stir frequently. Serves 6-8.

Spinach Sauté

> 4 tablespoons butter
> 1 cup minced onion
> 3 pounds spinach or 3 packages frozen (spinach to be cooked, drained and chopped)
> 1 clove garlic, minced
> ⅓ cup grated Parmesan cheese
> ⅓ cup dry bread crumbs
> ½ cup sour cream
> 2 tablespoons minced parsley

Melt the butter in a skillet; sauté the onion 10 minutes, stirring frequently. Add the spinach and garlic; sauté 3 minutes. Blend in the cheese, crumbs, sour cream and parsley. Heat, but do not let boil. Serves 6-8.

Spinaci alla Monachino
(Spinach, Monks Style)

> 3 pounds spinach, or 2 packages frozen
> 1 teaspoon salt
> ¼ cup olive oil
> 2 cloves garlic, minced
> 3 tablespoons pine nuts or sliced almonds
> ¼ cup sliced green olives
> ¼ cup sliced black olives
> 1 tablespoon capers
> 2 tablespoons seedless raisins

If fresh spinach is used, wash and drain. Sprinkle with the salt; cook 5 minutes, then drain and chop. If frozen spinach is used, cook 1 minute less than package directs. Drain and chop.

Heat the oil in a skillet; stir in the garlic and nuts until golden. Add the olives, capers and raisins, mixing until coated. Mix in the spinach; heat and serve. Serves 4-6.

Wilted Spinach

> 4 slices bacon
> 2 tablespoons water
> ⅓ cup cider vinegar
> 1½ tablespoons sugar
> 1 teaspoon salt
> ⅛ teaspoon pepper
> 2 packages frozen spinach, thawed

Fry the bacon crisp; drain and crumble. To the fat remaining, add the water, vinegar, sugar, salt and pepper. Bring to a boil and add the spinach. Cook over medium heat 3 minutes, stirring frequently. Sprinkle the bacon on top. Serves 4-6.

Braised Squash

    3 pounds yellow squash
    4 tablespoons butter
    ½ cup diced onions
    1½ teaspoons salt
    ¼ teaspoon pepper
    1 teaspoon sugar
    ½ cup sour cream (optional)

Wash the squash and slice paper thin. Combine in a saucepan with the butter, onions, salt, pepper and sugar. Cover and cook over low heat 30 minutes, stirring frequently. Mix in the sour cream, if desired. Serves 4-6.

Baked Acorn Squash

Split the squash; scrape out the seeds and fibers. Prick insides. Sprinkle each half with salt, a teaspoon of butter and a teaspoon of brown sugar or honey. Place in a shallow pan containing a little water. Cover the tops of the squash loosely with aluminum foil. Bake in a 375° oven 45-60 minutes, depending on the size. Remove the foil for the last 10 minutes.

Baked Acorn Squash with Bacon

    3 acorn squash
    6 tablespoons butter
    1¼ teaspoons salt
    6 teaspoons brown sugar
    3 slices bacon, diced

Cut the squash in half lengthwise; scoop out the seeds and fibers. Arrange on a baking pan, cut side up. Put 1 tablespoon of butter in each, season with the salt and 1 teaspoon brown sugar. Bake in a preheated 350° oven 30 minutes.

While the squash is baking, lightly brown the bacon.

Drain. Sprinkle the bacon in the squash halves. Bake 15 minutes longer, or until squash is tender when tested with a fork.

Broiled Tomatoes

> 4 large firm tomatoes
> 1½ teaspoons salt
> ¼ teaspoon freshly ground black pepper
> 4 tablespoons minced onion
> 2 tablespoons minced parsley
> 2 tablespoons butter or margarine

Remove the core from the stem end of the tomatoes; cut tomato in half crosswise. Sprinkle with the salt, pepper, onion and parsley. Dot with the butter. Broil until tender and browned (about 10 minutes), or bake in a 425° oven. Serves 4-8.

Curried Tomatoes

> 3 pounds firm tomatoes
> 3 tablespoons vegetable oil
> 2 cups thinly sliced onions
> 1 clove garlic, minced
> 1 teaspoon salt
> 2 teaspoons curry powder
> ¼ cup water

Wash, dry and quarter the tomatoes. Heat the oil in a skillet; sauté the onions 5 minutes. Mix in the garlic, salt and curry powder, then add the tomatoes and water. Cover and cook over low heat 15 minutes. Serves 6-8.

Tomato Fondue

> 1½ pounds tomatoes
> 2 tablespoons olive oil
> 3 tablespoons butter

¾ *cup thinly sliced onions*
1 *clove garlic, minced*
1¼ *teaspoons salt*
¼ *teaspoon freshly ground black pepper*
2 *tablespoons minced parsley*

Wash the tomatoes, remove cores and cut tomatoes in eighths. Heat the oil and butter in a saucepan; sauté the onions until yellow and transparent. Add the garlic, salt, pepper and tomatoes. Cover and cook over low heat 20 minutes, stirring frequently. Mix in the parsley. Serves 3-4.

Turnips, Chinese Style

8 *turnips*
4 *tablespoons vegetable oil*
½ *teaspoon salt*
1 *cup beef broth*
¼ *cup thinly sliced scallions (green onions)*
¼ *teaspoon freshly ground black pepper*
1 *tablespoon soy sauce*

Peel and grate the turnips coarsely. Heat the oil in a skillet; sauté the turnips 1 minute, stirring almost constantly. Add the salt and broth. Bring to a boil, cover and cook over low heat 5 minutes. Mix in the scallions, pepper and soy sauce. Cook uncovered 3 minutes. Serves 6-8.

Fried Zucchini

4 *zucchini (2 pounds)*
2½ *teaspoons salt*
¼ *teaspoon freshly ground black pepper*
¼ *cup dry bread crumbs*
¾ *cup flour*
Vegetable oil for deep frying

Buy young straight zucchini; wash and scrape lightly. Cut in 2-inch lengths, sliced pencil-thin. Sprinkle with 2 teaspoons salt and let stand 30 minutes. Drain well and dry on paper towels.

Mix together the pepper, bread crumbs, flour, and remaining salt. Toss the zucchini strips in the mixture. Heat the oil to 375°. Fry the zucchini until browned. Drain. Serves 4-6.

Zucchini Provençale

    4 tablespoons olive oil
    1 cup thinly sliced onions
    1 clove garlic, minced
    2 pounds zucchini, thinly sliced
    1 green pepper, cut in strips
    1 cup diced tomatoes
    1½ teaspoons salt
    ½ teaspoon freshly ground black pepper
    ½ teaspoon oregano

Heat the oil in a skillet; sauté the onions and garlic 5 minutes. Add the zucchini and green pepper; sauté 10 minutes, stirring frequently. Mix in the tomatoes, salt, pepper and oregano; cover and cook over low heat 20 minutes, mixing occasionally. Serves 6-8.

* * *

Green peas are surely among the oldest of all vegetables known to man. They probably first grew around the shores of the Mediterranean, where numerous findings have been made of dried peas in the excavations of burial places in Egypt and Greece. Archaeologists, finding some dried peas in an Egyptian tomb estimated to be over twenty five hundred years old, sent them to England. Botanists planted the old seeds and they sprouted successfully in English soil, many miles from their homeland, and many thousands of years after their normal life.

Vegetable Combinations

~~~~~~~~~~~~~~~~~~~~~~~~~~~~~~~~~

Artichauts à la Mirielle
(Artichokes with Onions)

⅓ cup olive or vegetable oil
12 small white onions
2 packages frozen artichoke hearts
⅓ cup chicken broth
1¼ teaspoons salt
¼ teaspoon freshly ground black pepper
1 cup peeled diced tomatoes
2 tablespoons minced parsley

Heat the oil in a deep skillet; sauté the onions 10 minutes, shaking the pan frequently. Add the artichoke hearts, broth, salt, pepper and tomatoes. Bring to a boil, cover and cook over low heat 15 minutes. Sprinkle with the parsley. Serves 6-8.

Artichauts à la Provençale
(Artichokes with Peas)

2 packages frozen artichoke hearts, thawed
4 tablespoons olive oil
1 clove garlic, minced
1 package frozen tiny green peas, thawed
1 cup shredded lettuce
1¼ teaspoons salt
⅛ teaspoon white pepper

Dry the artichokes on paper towels. Heat the oil in a skillet; lightly brown the artichokes in it. Add the garlic, peas, lettuce, salt and pepper. Cook over low heat 10 minutes, adding a very little water if necessary to keep from burning. Serves 8-10.

Bean Panache

> 1 package frozen lima beans
> 1 package frozen green beans
> 3 tablespoons butter
> 3 tablespoons minced onion
> 1 tablespoon lemon juice
> ⅛ teaspoon thyme
> 2 tablespoons minced parsley

Cook the beans separately as packages direct; drain well. While beans are cooking, melt the butter; sauté the onions 5 minutes. Add the lemon juice, thyme and parsley; toss with the beans. Serves 4-6.

Mixed Beans au Gratin

> 1 package frozen green beans
> 1 package frozen wax beans
> 1 package frozen lima beans
> 3 tablespoons butter
> 2 tablespoons grated onion
> 1½ tablespoons flour
> 1 teaspoon salt
> ⅛ teaspoon white pepper
> 1 cup heavy cream
> ½ cup grated Parmesan cheese

Cook the beans separately 1 minute less than packages direct; drain. Mix together lightly in a baking dish. Melt the butter in a saucepan; sauté the onion 2 minutes. Blend in the flour, salt and pepper. Gradually add the cream, stirring steadily to the boiling point; cook over low heat 5 minutes. Pour over the beans and sprinkle with the cheese. Bake in a preheated 375° oven 10 minutes or until browned. Serves 8-10.

Green Beans, Mushrooms and Almonds

> 1½ pounds green beans, or 2 packages frozen green
>   beans
> 3 tablespoons butter
> ½ cup chopped onion
> ½ pound mushrooms, sliced
> 1¼ teaspoons salt
> ⅛ teaspoon white pepper
> ¼ cup sliced almonds
> 3 tablespoons heavy cream

Cook the beans until tender but firm; drain. Melt the butter in a skillet; sauté the onion 5 minutes. Add the mushrooms; sauté 4 minutes. Mix in the salt, pepper and almonds; cook 1 minute. Add the cream to the beans; bring to a boil. Place in a serving dish with the mushroom mixture on top. Serves 6-8.

Brussels Sprouts with Mushrooms

> 2 pounds Brussels sprouts, or 2 packages frozen
> 2 teaspoons salt
> 4 tablespoons butter
> ¼ pound mushrooms, sliced
> 2 tablespoons chopped onion
> 1 tablespoon lemon juice
> ⅛ teaspoon freshly ground black pepper

Wash the fresh sprouts and trim them. Soak in salted water for 10 minutes; rinse and drain. Place in a saucepan; add boiling water to a depth of 1 inch and 1 teaspoon salt. Cook over low heat 5 minutes. Cover pan and cook 10 minutes longer, or until tender. Drain. If frozen sprouts are used, cook ½ minute less than package directs. While the sprouts are cooking, prepare the mushrooms.

Melt the butter in a skillet; sauté the mushrooms and onion 5 minutes. Add the lemon juice, pepper and remaining salt; toss with the sprouts. Serves 6-8.

Brussels Sprouts with Chestnuts

    1 pound chestnuts
    1 cup beef broth
    2 packages frozen Brussels sprouts
    ¼ pound butter
    1 teaspoon salt
    ¼ teaspoon pepper

Cut a crisscross in the pointed end of the chestnuts and bake in a 375° oven 15 minutes. Cool and remove the shells. Cook the chestnuts in the broth 10 minutes, or until tender. Drain well. Cook the sprouts as package directs; drain. Melt the butter in a skillet; add the chestnuts, tossing until well coated. Lightly mix in the sprouts, salt and pepper. Serves 8-10.

Celery and Tomatoes

    3 tablespoons butter
    ½ cup minced onion
    4 cups sliced celery
    2 cups diced tomatoes
    1½ teaspoons salt
    ¼ teaspoon pepper
    2 tablespoons minced parsley

Melt the butter in a skillet; sauté the onion 5 minutes. Add the celery; sauté 5 minutes. Mix in the tomatoes, salt and pepper. Cover and cook over low heat 10 minutes. Sprinkle with the parsley. Serves 4-6.

Chinese Corn and Chicken

    1 raw chicken breast
    1¼ teaspoons salt
    1 teaspoon cornstarch
    1 teaspoon soy sauce
    1 12-ounce can cream-style corn
    1 cup water
    2 egg whites

Remove the skin and bones of the chicken breast. Chop fine or grind. Mix with the salt, cornstarch and soy sauce.

Bring to a boil the undrained corn and the water (reserving 1 tablespoon). Mix in the chicken mixture, stirring constantly to prevent lumps from forming. Cook over low heat 10 minutes. Beat the egg whites and remaining water; stir into the corn mixture gradually. Cook 30 seconds. Serve with rice or noodles. Serves 2-4.

Eggplant and Asparagus Mornay

> 6 slices eggplant, cut ½ inch thick
> 3 teaspoons salt
> ⅛ teaspoon freshly ground black pepper
> ¼ cup flour
> ½ cup vegetable oil
> 24 asparagus stalks, washed and drained

Sprinkle the eggplant slices with 2 teaspoons salt and the pepper; dip in the flour. Heat the oil in a skillet; brown the eggplant on both sides. Transfer to a heated serving dish and keep warm. Cook the asparagus in ½ inch of boiling water with the remaining salt 12 minutes, or until tender. Drain; place 4 asparagus stalks on each slice of eggplant. Cover with the following sauce:

> 2 tablespoons butter
> 1 tablespoon flour
> ½ teaspoon salt
> ⅛ teaspoon freshly ground black pepper
> 1 cup milk
> ½ cup grated Cheddar cheese
> ¼ cup grated Parmesan cheese
> 1 teaspoon lemon juice

Melt the butter in a saucepan; blend in the flour, salt and pepper. Add the milk, stirring steadily to the boiling point; cook over low heat 10 minutes. Mix in the cheeses and lemon juice, stirring until melted. Spoon over the vegetables. Serves 6.

Eggplant-Zucchini Melange

> 1 medium eggplant
> 3 teaspoons salt
> 1/3 cup olive oil
> 2 cups thinly sliced zucchini
> 1/4 cup finely chopped onion
> 1 clove garlic, minced
> 4 tablespoons dry bread crumbs
> 2 tablespoons minced parsley
> 1/4 pound mushrooms, sliced and sautéed

Peel the eggplant and cut in 1-inch cubes. Sprinkle with 1½ teaspoons salt and let stand 30 minutes. Drain well and dry. Heat 2 tablespoons oil in a skillet; brown the eggplant cubes on all sides. Remove and keep warm.

Heat 2 tablespoons oil in the skillet; sauté the zucchini 10 minutes, or until tender. Season with 1 teaspoon salt. Add to the eggplant.

Heat the remaining oil in the skillet; sauté the onion 3 minutes. Mix in the garlic, bread crumbs, parsley and remaining salt. Cook over low heat 2 minutes, stirring constantly. Mix in the mushrooms, then spread over the eggplant and zucchini. Serves 6-8.

Fennel and Chard au Gratin

> 1½ pounds chard
> 6 bulbs fennel
> 4 tablespoons dry bread crumbs
> 2 cups medium white sauce
> 1/4 cup grated Parmesan cheese
> 1/4 cup grated Swiss cheese
> 2 tablespoons butter

Wash the chard thoroughly, cut away the stalks and tear the leaves coarsely. Trim the fennel of the stalks and leaves; cut the bulbs in 1-inch pieces. Cook the chard and fennel in boiling salted water 10 minutes. Drain well.

Sprinkle half the bread crumbs on the bottom of a

buttered casserole. Spread the drained vegetables over them; cover with the white sauce. Sprinkle top with a mixture of the Parmesan and Swiss cheese and remaining bread crumbs. Dot with the butter.

Bake in a 350° oven 20 minutes, or until browned. Serves 4-6.

Leeks and Tomato Sauce

> *18 leeks*
> *4 tablespoons olive oil*
> *1 cup chopped onion*
> *½ cup grated carrots*
> *1 cup chopped tomatoes*
> *1 teaspoon salt*
> *¼ teaspoon freshly ground black pepper*
> *⅛ teaspoon basil*

Trim the leeks, cutting away the roots and most of the green part. Wash very carefully to remove all the earth. Cut in 1-inch lengths.

Heat the oil in a skillet; sauté the onion 10 minutes. Mix in the carrots, tomatoes, salt, pepper and basil; cook over low heat 5 minutes. Add the leeks; cook over low heat 20 minutes, or until leeks are tender. Serves 4-6.

Setas con Alcachofas
(Mushrooms and Artichokes)

> *4 tablespoons butter*
> *2 packages frozen artichoke hearts, thawed*
> *1 pound mushrooms, sliced*
> *1¼ teaspoons salt*
> *¼ teaspoon freshly ground black pepper*
> *¼ teaspoon thyme*
> *¼ cup dry sherry*
> *¼ cup chicken broth*

Melt the butter in a skillet; sauté the artichoke hearts 3 minutes. Add the mushrooms; sauté 2 minutes. Season with the salt, pepper and thyme; add the sherry and broth. Cook over medium heat 5 minutes. Serves 6-8.

Okra and Corn

> 1 pound okra, or 1 package frozen, thawed
> 4 tablespoons butter
> ½ cup minced onion
> 1½ cups fresh or frozen corn kernels
> ¾ cup beef broth or water
> 1 teaspoon salt
> ¼ teaspoon freshly ground black pepper

Cut the okra in ½-inch pieces. Melt the butter in a skillet; sauté the onion 5 minutes. Mix in the okra and corn; cook over low heat 5 minutes, stirring frequently. Add the broth, salt and pepper; cover and cook over low heat 20 minutes. Serves 3-4.

Legumes à la Nivernaise
(Peas and Carrots in Cream)

> 6 tablespoons butter
> 1 cup shredded lettuce
> 6 scallions (green onions), sliced
> 2 packages frozen peas and carrots, thawed
> 1 package frozen peas, thawed
> ¼ cup water
> 1½ teaspoons salt
> ½ teaspoon sugar
> ½ cup heavy cream

Melt the butter in a deep skillet. Spread the lettuce and scallions on the bottom and add the peas and carrots, peas, water, salt and sugar. Bring to a boil, cover and cook over low heat 15 minutes, shaking the pan frequently. Mix in the cream; cook 2 minutes. Serves 6-8.

Green Pepper and Mushroom Sauté

> 3 tablespoons olive oil
> 1 cup thinly sliced onions
> 3 green peppers, cut in thin rings
> ½ pound mushrooms, sliced
> 1¼ teaspoons salt
> ¼ teaspoon freshly ground black pepper
> ⅛ teaspoon oregano

Heat the oil in a skillet; sauté the onions 5 minutes. Add the green peppers; sauté 5 minutes, stirring frequently. Mix in the mushrooms, salt, pepper and oregano; cook over low heat 5 minutes, stirring frequently. Serves 4-6.

Squash and Tomatoes

> 2 pounds small yellow squash
> ¼ cup olive oil
> 1½ cups chopped onion
> 4 tomatoes, peeled and chopped
> ½ cup water
> 1½ teaspoons salt
> ⅛ teaspoon white pepper
> 1 tablespoon minced parsley
> 4 tablespoons grated Parmesan cheese

Scrape the squash and cut into 1-inch cubes. Heat the oil in a skillet; brown the onion in it. Add the tomatoes, water, salt and pepper. Bring to a boil and cook over low heat 5 minutes. Add the squash; cover and cook over low heat 30 minutes. Shake the skillet frequently. Sprinkle with parsley and the cheese. Serves 4-6.

Succotash

>   3 tablespoons butter
>   2 cups cooked (firm) lima beans
>   3 cups corn kernels, fresh or canned
>   2 teaspoons grated onion
>   1/3 cup light cream
>   1 teaspoon salt
>   1/4 teaspoon white pepper
>   2 teaspoons sugar

Combine all the ingredients in a saucepan; cook over low heat 15 minutes. Serves 6-8.

NOTE: Succotash is available frozen; use 2 packages. Cook half as long as package directs, then drain and add all the other ingredients listed. Cook 15 minutes.

Mixed Chinese Vegetables

>   1 pound Chinese celery cabbage
>   1/2 pound bean sprouts, fresh or canned
>   3 tablespoons vegetable oil
>   3 bamboo shoots, sliced
>   1/2 pound snow peas, or 1 package frozen
>   6 water chestnuts, sliced
>   1 teaspoon salt
>   1/4 teaspoon Ac'cent
>   1/2 teaspoon sugar
>   1/4 cup water

Wash the celery cabbage and slice thin, diagonally. (If not available, use celery or cabbage.) Wash the fresh sprouts, or drain the canned ones.

Heat the oil in a large skillet. Add the celery cabbage, bean sprouts, bamboo shoots, snow peas, water chestnuts, salt, Ac'cent and sugar. Cook over high heat 1 minute, stirring constantly. Add the water; cover and cook 3 minutes. The vegetables should be crisp.

Vegetables in Sauces

Sweet and Sour Beans

   2 pounds green or wax beans, or 2 packages frozen
   4 slices bacon, diced
   ½ cup chopped onions
   ¼ cup cider vinegar
   1 tablespoon sugar
   ½ teaspoon Ac'cent
   2 tablespoons minced parsley

Cook the beans in salted water until tender. Drain, reserving the liquid. Fry the bacon and onion until onions are tender. Add the bean liquid and cook until reduced to ¼ cup. Mix in the vinegar, sugar and Ac'cent. Cook over low heat 5 minutes. Stir in the beans. Heat and taste for seasoning. Sprinkle with the parsley. Serves 6-8.

Green Beans in Spring Sauce

   3 tablespoons olive oil
   ¾ cup finely chopped onion
   2 cloves garlic, minced
   2 tomatoes, peeled and chopped
   1 teaspoon grated lemon rind
   1½ teaspoons salt
   ⅛ teaspoon Tabasco
   ½ teaspoon sugar
   ¾ cup light cream
   2 pounds green beans cut French style or 2 packages
     frozen, thawed

Heat the oil in a saucepan; sauté the onion, garlic and tomato 3 minutes, stirring frequently. Add the lemon rind, salt, Tabasco, sugar, cream and beans. Bring to a boil, cover loosely and cook over low heat 15 minutes, or until beans are tender. Serve hot or cold. Serves 6-8.

Green Beans, Italian Style

> 3 tablespoons olive oil
> ½ cup chopped onion
> 1 clove garlic, minced
> 1 20-ounce can tomatoes, drained
> 1 teaspoon salt
> ½ teaspoon freshly ground black pepper
> ¼ teaspoon oregano
> 1 bay leaf
> 2 pounds green beans, or 3 packages frozen, thawed

Heat the oil in a saucepan; sauté the onion 10 minutes. Add the garlic, tomatoes, salt, pepper, oregano and bay leaf; bring to a boil and cook over low heat 20 minutes.

If using fresh beans, cut in thirds. Add the fresh or frozen beans to the tomato mixture. Cover and cook over low heat 30 minutes. Taste for seasoning. Serves 6-8.

Green Beans, Swiss Style

> 2 pounds cooked or canned green beans
> 4 eggs
> 1 teaspoon salt
> ¼ teaspoon freshly ground black pepper
> 3 tablespoons minced onion
> 2 cups grated Swiss cheese
> ½ cup drained cottage cheese

Spread half the drained beans on the bottom of a buttered 2-quart baking dish. Beat together the eggs, salt and pepper. Mix in the onion, Swiss cheese and cottage cheese; pour half over the beans. Repeat the layers. Bake in a preheated 350° oven 35 minutes, or until set and browned. Serves 6-8.

Green Beans in Sour Cream Sauce

    2 pounds green beans, cut, or 2 packages frozen
    3 tablespoons butter
    ¼ cup chopped onion
    1 clove garlic, minced
    2 tablespoons flour
    1 teaspoon salt
    2 teaspoons paprika
    2 tablespoons minced parsley
    1 cup sour cream
    1 teaspoon lemon juice
    2 teaspoons sugar

Cook the beans in boiling, salted water until tender but still firm. Drain, reserving ¼ cup liquid.

Melt the butter in a skillet; sauté the onion 5 minutes. Mix in the garlic and flour until browned. Stir in the salt, paprika, parsley and reserved liquid, then add the beans, sour cream, lemon juice and sugar. Heat, but do not let boil. Serves 6-8.

Haricots Verts à la Niçoise
(Green Beans, Riviera Style)

    ¼ cup olive oil
    1 cup chopped onion
    1 clove garlic, minced
    ¼ cup chopped green pepper
    1½ cups peeled diced tomatoes
    2 teaspoons salt
    ¼ teaspoon freshly ground black pepper
    1 bay leaf
    1½ pounds green beans or 2 packages frozen, thawed
    ¼ teaspoon sugar
    2 tablespoons minced parsley

Heat the oil in a deep skillet; sauté the onion, garlic and green pepper 5 minutes. Add the tomatoes, salt, pepper and bay leaf. Bring to a boil and cook over low heat 10 minutes.

Cut the fresh or frozen beans in quarters. Add the beans, sugar and parsley. Cover and cook over low heat 25 minutes. Serves 4-6.

Haricots Verts Portugaise
(Green Beans, Portuguese Style)

3 slices salt pork or bacon, diced
1 cup peeled chopped tomatoes
1½ pounds green beans, cut, or 2 packages frozen, thawed
¾ cup beef broth
1 teaspoon salt
¼ teaspoon freshly ground black pepper
2 tablespoons minced parsley

Lightly brown the salt pork in a skillet; pour off the fat. Add the tomatoes, beans, broth, salt and pepper. Cover and cook over low heat 30 minutes. Drain, if any liquid remains. Sprinkle with the parsley. Serves 4-6.

Haricots Verts Béarnaise
(Green Beans Béarnaise)

1½ pounds green beans, or 2 packages frozen
3 tablespoons butter
½ cup diced ham
1 cup peeled diced tomatoes
1 clove garlic, minced
1 teaspoon salt
¼ teaspoon freshly ground black pepper

Cut the fresh beans in quarters; cook in boiling salted water 10 minutes, or until tender but crisp. Drain. Cook the frozen beans 1½ minutes less than package directs; drain.

Melt the butter in a skillet; sauté the ham 2 minutes. Add the beans, tomatoes, garlic, salt and pepper. Cover and cook over low heat 10 minutes, shaking the pan frequently. Serves 4-6.

Lima Beans in Sour Cream Sauce

>   2 packages frozen lima beans
>   ¾ cup sour cream
>   ½ cup dry white wine
>   ⅛ teaspoon white pepper
>   ¼ cup minced pimientos
>   2 tablespoons minced parsley

Cook the lima beans ½ minute less than package directs. Drain well. Mix together the sour cream, wine and pepper. Add to the beans with the pimientos. Cook over low heat 5 minutes, but do not let boil. Taste for seasoning. Sprinkle with the parsley and serve. Serves 4-6.

Lima Beans in Paprika Sauce

>   2 packages frozen lima beans
>   3 tablespoons butter
>   ½ cup thinly sliced scallions (green onions)
>   1 tablespoon flour
>   1 teaspoon salt
>   ¼ teaspoon pepper
>   1 teaspoon paprika
>   ½ cup sour cream

Cook the beans as package directs; drain, reserving ½ cup liquid. Melt the butter in a saucepan; sauté the scallions 5 minutes. Blend in the flour, salt and pepper; add the liquid, stirring constantly to the boiling point. Cook over low heat 5 minutes. Blend in the paprika and sour cream, then add the beans. Heat, but do not let boil. Serves 4-6.

Beets in Orange Sauce

½ cup orange juice
2 teaspoons lemon juice
3 tablespoons butter
1 teaspoon salt
4 cups shredded fresh beets, or drained canned
2 teaspoons cornstarch

Combine the orange juice (reserving 1 tablespoon), lemon juice, butter and salt in a saucepan. Bring to a boil and add the beets; cover and cook over low heat 10 minutes for fresh beets, or until tender; 5 minutes for canned beets. Mix the cornstarch with the reserved orange juice; stir into the beets until thickened and clear. Serves 4-6.

Beets with Horseradish Sauce

3 cups grated beets
2 cups water
1 tablespoon cider vinegar
½ teaspoon salt
2 tablespoons butter
2 tablespoons flour
1 cup light cream
3 tablespoons prepared horseradish

In a saucepan, combine the beets, water, vinegar and salt. Bring to a boil and cook over low heat 10 minutes. Drain, reserving the liquid.

Melt the butter in a saucepan; blend in the flour. Gradually add the beet liquid and cream, stirring steadily to the boiling point. Cook over low heat 5 minutes. Mix in the horseradish, then the beets. Serves 6-8.

Broccoli, Sicilian Style

1 large bunch broccoli, or 2 packages frozen
1 teaspoon salt

2 tablespoons olive oil
½ cup thinly sliced onions
1 clove garlic, minced
1½ tablespoons flour
4 teaspoons freshly ground black pepper
1 cup chicken broth
1 cup grated Mozzarella or white American cheese
4 anchovies, minced
½ cup sliced black olives (Italian, if available)

Wash the fresh broccoli thoroughly. Remove the coarse leaves and tough lower portions of the stalks. Split lengthwise. Place in a skillet with the salt and boiling water to a depth of ½-inch. Bring to a boil and cook over low heat 5 minutes. Cover and cook over low heat 15 minutes, or until tender. Drain and keep hot. Cook frozen broccoli 1 minute less than package directs; drain and keep hot.

Prepare the sauce while the vegetable is cooking. Heat the oil in a saucepan; sauté the onions and garlic 5 minutes. Blend in the flour and pepper. Gradually add the broth, stirring steadily to the boiling point; cook over low heat 5 minutes. Mix in the cheese until melted, then stir in the anchovies and olives. Pour over the broccoli. Serves 4-6.

Broccoli with Lemon Butter Sauce

2 packages frozen broccoli
¼ cup melted butter or margarine
3 tablespoons lemon juice
½ teaspoon salt
⅛ teaspoon pepper
1 hard-cooked egg yolk, grated

Cook the broccoli 1 minute less than package directs; drain. Heat together the butter, lemon juice, salt and pepper; pour over the broccoli and sprinkle with the egg yolk. Serves 4-6.

Creole Cabbage

  3 tablespoons butter
  2 cups thinly sliced onions
  1 green pepper, cut in strips
  1½ cups diced tomatoes
  1 2-pound cabbage, cut in chunks
  1½ teaspoons salt
  ¼ teaspoon pepper
  ¼ teaspoon thyme

Melt the butter in a saucepan; sauté the onions 5 minutes. Add the green pepper; sauté 5 minutes. Add the tomatoes, cabbage, salt, pepper and thyme. Cover and cook over low heat 25 minutes, or until tender. Watch carefully and add a little boiling water if necessary. Serves 4-6.

Cabbage with Sour Cream Sauce

  1 3-pound cabbage
  2 tablespoons butter
  ¼ cup minced onion
  1 tablespoon flour
  2 teaspoons cider vinegar
  1 cup sour cream
  1 teaspoon salt
  ⅛ teaspoon pepper
  ½ teaspoon sugar

Cut the cabbage in 4 wedges. Cook in boiling salted water 12 minutes, or until tender. Drain well. Prepare the sauce while the cabbage is cooking.

Melt the butter in a saucepan; sauté the onion 5 minutes. Blend in the flour. Add the vinegar, sour cream, salt, pepper and sugar. Cook over low heat, stirring steadily until thickened. Pour over the cabbage. Sprinkle with paprika if desired. Serves 4.

Sweet and Sour Red Cabbage

> *3 tablespoons butter*
> *½ cup chopped onion*
> *8 cups shredded red cabbage*
> *1 apple, peeled and diced*
> *1 cup water*
> *3 tablespoons cider vinegar*
> *2 tablespoons sugar*
> *1½ teaspoons salt*
> *¼ teaspoon pepper*
> *¼ cup seedless raisins (optional)*

Melt the butter in a saucepan; sauté the onion 5 minutes. Mix in the cabbage; cover and cook over low heat 5 minutes. Add the apple, water, vinegar, sugar, salt and pepper. Cover and cook over low heat 30 minutes, stirring frequently. Add the raisins, if desired; cook 5 minutes longer. Serves 4-6.

Cabbage with Cheese Sauce

> *1 3-pound cabbage*
> *1½ teaspoons salt*
> *4 cups water*
> *2 cups white sauce, medium thick*
> *1 cup grated Cheddar cheese*
> *4 slices crisp bacon, crumbled (optional)*

Cut the cabbage in 8 wedges. Salt the water and bring to a boil; add the cabbage. Cook over medium heat 10 minutes, or until tender but still crisp; drain well. Combine the white sauce and cheese; cook over low heat, stirring steadily until cheese melts. Pour over the cabbage and sprinkle with the bacon, if desired. Serves 4-6.

Creamed Cabbage

> *2 tablespoons butter*
> *6 cups finely shredded cabbage*

1 cup water
1 cup sour cream
1½ teaspoons salt
¼ teaspoon pepper
½ teaspoon caraway seeds

Melt the butter in a saucepan; sauté the cabbage 5 minutes, stirring frequently. Add the water; cover and cook over low heat 10 minutes. Drain. Mix in the sour cream, salt, pepper and caraway seeds; cook over low heat 5 minutes. Serves 4-6.

Creamed Carrots

3 tablespoons butter
5 cups grated carrots
1 teaspoon salt
1 tablespoon sugar
2 teaspoons cornstarch
½ cup heavy cream

Melt the butter in a saucepan; mix in the carrots, salt and sugar. Cover and cook over low heat 10 minutes, stirring frequently. Mix the cornstarch and cream. Add to the carrots, stirring steadily to the boiling point. Cover and cook over low heat 5 minutes. Serves 4-6.

Sweet and Sour Carrots

10 carrots
1½ cups water
¾ teaspoon salt
2 tablespoons butter
2 teaspoons flour
1 tablespoon sugar
1 tablespoon vinegar

Wash, scrape and thinly slice the carrots. Combine in a saucepan with the water and salt; bring to a boil and cook over low heat 10 minutes. Drain, reserving 1 cup of the liquid.

Melt the butter in a saucepan; blend in the flour. Add the liquid, stirring steadily to the boiling point. Mix in the sugar, vinegar and carrots. Cook over low heat 5 minutes. Serves 4-6.

Cavolfiore alla Milanese
(Cauliflower with Cheese)

> *1 medium-sized cauliflower, or 2 packages frozen*
> *½ cup grated Swiss cheese*
> *2 tablespoons grated Parmesan cheese*
> *¼ cup melted butter*
> *2 tablespoons dry bread crumbs*

Remove the leaves of the fresh cauliflower and wash thoroughly. Cook in boiling salted water 15 minutes, or until tender but firm. Drain. Cook the frozen cauliflower 2 minutes less than package directs. Drain.

Place the cauliflower in a baking dish. Mix together the Swiss cheese, Parmesan cheese, butter and bread crumbs; spread over the cauliflower. Bake in a 425° oven 5 minutes, or until browned. Serves 4-6.

Choux-Fleurs à la Normande
(Cauliflower in Cider Sauce)

> *3 tablespoons butter*
> *1 tablespoon flour*
> *1 teaspoon salt*
> *⅛ teaspoon white pepper*
> *½ cup apple cider*
> *½ cup heavy cream*
> *1 medium cauliflower, cooked and drained*

Melt the butter in a saucepan; stir in the flour, salt and pepper. Mix together the cider and cream. Add to the

butter mixture, stirring steadily to the boiling point.
Cook over low heat 5 minutes.

Place the cauliflower in a serving dish and pour the
sauce over it. Serves 4-6.

Kounoupithi Yahni
(Cauliflower, Greek Style)

> *1 large cauliflower, or 2 packages frozen, thawed*
> *¼ cup vegetable oil*
> *1½ cups chopped onion*
> *2 cloves garlic, minced*
> *2 cups puréed canned tomatoes*
> *1½ teaspoons salt*
> *½ teaspoon freshly ground black pepper*
> *¼ cup chopped parsley*

Wash the fresh cauliflower and separate into flowerets.
Heat the oil in a saucepan; brown the onion in it. Add
the garlic, tomatoes, salt and pepper. Bring to a boil and
cook over low heat 10 minutes. Add the fresh or frozen
cauliflower. Cook fresh cauliflower 20 minutes; frozen 10
minutes. Sprinkle with parsley. Serves 4-6.

Celery Parmigiana

> *3 bunches celery*
> *3 tablespoons butter*
> *½ cup beef broth*
> *1 teaspoon salt*
> *¼ teaspoon freshly ground black pepper*
> *¼ cup chopped ham*
> *¼ cup grated Swiss cheese*
> *¼ cup grated Parmesan cheese*

Wash the celery and discard the leaves. Cut into ½-inch
pieces. Melt the butter in a skillet; sauté the celery 5
minutes, shaking the pan frequently. Add the broth,
salt, pepper and ham. Cover and cook over low heat 15

minutes, stirring frequently. Drain if any liquid remains. Turn into a buttered baking dish; sprinkle with the mixed cheeses. Bake in a 425° oven 10 minutes, or until browned. Serves 6-8.

Celery with Almond Sauce

    2 bunches celery
    4 tablespoons butter
    2 tablespoons grated onion
    1¼ teaspoons salt
    ⅛ teaspoon white pepper
    1 tablespoon flour
    ⅓ cup chicken broth
    ¾ cup light cream
    ½ cup sliced toasted blanched almonds

Cut the celery bunches in half lengthwise and discard the leaves; cut into ½-inch pieces. Melt the butter in a deep skillet. Add the celery, onion, salt and pepper. Cover and cook over low heat 25 minutes, or until tender. Stir frequently and watch carefully to prevent burning.

Mix together the flour, broth and cream. Add to the celery, stirring steadily to the boiling point; cook over low heat 5 minutes. Taste for seasoning, mix in the almonds and serve. Serves 3-4.

Leafy Greens with Sour Cream

    1½ pounds kale, turnip or mustard greens
    1½ cups water
    1½ teaspoons salt
    ¾ cup sour cream
    2 tablespoons chopped scallion (green onions)

Wash the greens thoroughly and remove any tough stalks. Chop the greens coarsely. Bring the water and salt to a boil. Add the greens; cover and cook over medium heat 10 minutes, or until tender. Drain well and toss with the sour cream. Sprinkle with the scallions. Serves 4-6.

Poireaux en Hachis
(Leeks in Cream)

> 24 leeks
> 1½ cups heavy cream
> 1 teaspoon salt
> ¼ teaspoon freshly ground black pepper
> 1 egg yolk, beaten

Trim the leeks, cutting away the roots and most of the green. Wash very carefully to remove all the earth. Cut in pieces, then cook in boiling salted water 8 minutes. Drain well and chop.

Combine the leeks, cream, salt and pepper in the top of a double boiler. Cook over hot water 20 minutes, or until the leeks are tender. Add a little of the hot mixture to the egg yolk, mixing steadily to prevent curdling. Return to the top of the double boiler. Heat, but do not let boil. Serves 4-6.

Mushrooms and Tomatoes in Cream Sauce

> 1 pound mushrooms, sliced
> ¼ pound butter
> 1½ teaspoons salt
> ½ teaspoon freshly ground black pepper
> 4 firm tomatoes
> ⅓ cup flour
> 1½ tablespoons brown sugar
> 1 cup light cream

Sauté the mushrooms in a skillet in 3 tablespoons butter. Season with half the salt and pepper. Remove from the pan. Cut each tomato in 3 slices. Dip in the flour, reserving 2 tablespoons.

Melt 3 tablespoons butter in the skillet; brown the tomatoes on one side, then turn. Sprinkle with the sugar and remaining salt and pepper. Brown the undersides. Remove from the pan.

Melt the remaining butter in the skillet; blend in the

reserved flour. Gradually add the cream, stirring steadily to the boiling point. Cook over low heat 3 minutes. Return the mushrooms and tomatoes; taste for seasoning. Serve in the center of a noodle ring, or as is. Serves 6-8.

Parsnips in Cheese Sauce

> 8 parsnips
> 1 cup white sauce, medium thick
> ¾ cup grated Cheddar or American cheese

Scrub the parsnips and cook in boiling salted water 20 minutes. Drain and peel. Slice thin and arrange in a buttered shallow baking dish. Cook the white sauce and cheese over low heat until cheese melts. Pour over the parsnips until browned. Serves 4-6.

Peperoni alla Romana
(Green Peppers in Tomato Sauce)

> 4 tablespoons olive oil
> 2 cups coarsely chopped onions
> 4 cups coarsely chopped green peppers
> 1 8-ounce can tomato sauce
> 1½ teaspoons salt
> ¼ teaspoon freshly ground black pepper
> ¼ teaspoon rosemary
> 2 tablespoons minced parsley

Heat the oil in a skillet; sauté the onions 10 minutes. Add the peppers, tomato sauce, salt, pepper and rosemary. Cook over low heat 25 minutes, or until peppers are tender. Sprinkle with the parsley. Serves 4-6.

VARIATION: Substitute 1 cup dry white wine for the tomato sauce. Omit rosemary.

Puréed Pumpkin with Sour Cream

> 4 pounds pumpkin
> ¼ cup water

2 tablespoons raw rice
1½ teaspoons salt
1 tablespoon sugar
4 tablespoons butter
¾ cup sour cream

Peel the pumpkin, remove the seeds and fibers, and dice. In a heavy saucepan, combine the pumpkin, water, rice and salt. Cook over low heat 45 minutes, or until tender, mixing frequently. The vegetable should be dry at this point; if not, drain.

Mash the pumpkin; stir in the sugar, butter and sour cream. Cook over low heat 10 minutes, stirring frequently. Serves 4-6.

NOTE: Yellow (summer) squash may be prepared in the same manner.

Sorrel with Sour Cream

2 pounds sorrel (sour grass)
3 tablespoons butter
1 cup chopped onion
1¼ teaspoons salt
2 tablespoons flour
1 cup sour cream
2 tablespoons sugar

Clean sorrel, remove stems, wash and drain. Melt the butter in a deep skillet; sauté the onion 10 minutes. Add the sorrel and salt; cover and cook over low heat 10 minutes. Add the flour mixed with the sour cream; cook over low heat 10 minutes. Purée in an electric blender or force through a sieve. Stir in the sugar and return to skillet; cook over low heat 10 minutes. Serves 3-4.

Creamed Spinach

2 packages frozen spinach
3 tablespoons butter
3 tablespoons grated onion

1 tablespoon flour
1 teaspoon salt
⅛ teaspoon pepper
⅛ teaspoon nutmeg
¾ cup light cream

Cook the spinach as package directs. Drain; purée in an electric blender or chop very fine. Melt the butter in a saucepan; blend in the onion, flour, salt, pepper and nutmeg. Add the cream, stirring steadily to the boiling point. Cook over low heat 5 minutes. Mix in the spinach; heat. Serves 4-6.

Spinach-Rice Nests

4 tablespoons butter
¼ cup chopped onion
2 cups cooked chopped spinach, drained
2 cups cooked rice
1½ teaspoons salt
¼ teaspoon freshly ground black pepper
½ cup grated Cheddar cheese

Melt the butter in a skillet; sauté the onion 5 minutes. Stir in the spinach, rice, salt, pepper and cheese. Cook over low heat, stirring steadily until cheese melts.

Shape into 4-6 mounds. Served with a poached egg on top, the nests make a delicious luncheon or supper dish. Serves 4-6.

Cheese-Stuffed Tomatoes

4 large firm tomatoes
¼ cup dry bread crumbs
½ cup grated Parmesan cheese
¾ cup grated Swiss cheese
3 tablespoons chopped scallions (green onions)
4 tablespoons melted butter

Wash the tomatoes, cut in half crosswise, and hollow centers slightly. Mix together the bread crumbs, cheeses and scallions; divide evenly among the tomato halves. Arrange in buttered baking dish; sprinkle with the butter. Bake in a 350° oven 15 minutes. Serves 4-8.

Turnips in Sherry Sauce

> 3 pounds turnips
> 3 tablespoons butter
> 2 tablespoons minced onion
> ½ cup sliced mushrooms
> 2 tablespoons flour
> 1¼ teaspoons salt
> ⅛ teaspoon white pepper
> ½ cup heavy cream
> ¾ cup chicken broth
> ¼ cup dry sherry
> 1 egg yolk
> 2 tablespoons minced parsley

Peel the turnips; cut into ½-inch slices, and then into ½-inch strips. Cook in 1 inch of boiling salted water 5 minutes, then cover and cook 12 minutes longer, or until tender. Drain well. Prepare the sauce while the turnips are cooking.

Melt the butter in a saucepan; sauté the onion and mushrooms 5 minutes. Blend in the flour, salt and pepper. Add the cream and broth, stirring steadily to the boiling point; cook over low heat 5 minutes. Beat the sherry and egg yolk in a bowl; gradually add a little of the hot sauce, stirring steadily to prevent curdling. Return to saucepan, heat, but do not let boil. Toss with the turnips. Sprinkle with the parsley. Serves 6-8.

NOTE: Parsnips may be prepared in the same manner.

*   *   *

Celery is a vegetable developed from a very ordinary English weed, commonly seen throughout the countryside, called "smallage." It is closely related to the dill and parsley family of vegetables.

Potato Recipes

Potatoes in Parsley Butter

6 potatoes
2 teaspoons salt
2 cups water
4 tablespoons butter
4 tablespoons minced parsley

Peel the potatoes and cut in 2-inch cubes. Bring the salt and water to a boil. Add the potatoes and cook over medium heat 10 minutes, or until tender. Drain well.

Melt the butter in the same saucepan. Add the potatoes and parsley; toss until potatoes are well coated. Serves 6.

Alsatian Potato Puffs

5 cups mashed potatoes
(2 pounds or 3 envelopes instant potatoes)
4 tablespoons melted butter
2 eggs, beaten
3 tablespoons flour
3 tablespoons grated onion
1 clove garlic, minced
2 tablespoons minced parsley
1½ teaspoons salt
¼ teaspoon white pepper
¼ teaspoon nutmeg

Beat together all the ingredients until light and fluffy. Drop by the heaping tablespoon onto a buttered baking pan. Bake in a 375° oven 10 minutes, or until browned. Serve with browned butter if desired. Serves 6-8.

Potatoes Lyonnaise

>   5 potatoes (2 pounds)
>   5 tablespoons butter
>   1 cup thinly sliced onions
>   1½ teaspoons salt
>   ¼ teaspoon freshly ground black pepper
>   1 tablespoon minced parsley

Cook the unpeeled potatoes in boiling water until just tender. Drain, slip off the skins and slice.

Melt 2 tablespoons butter in a skillet; lightly brown the onions. Remove. Melt the remaining butter in the skillet; brown the potatoes. Toss in the onions, salt and pepper; cook over low heat 3 minutes. Sprinkle with the parsley. Serves 4-6.

Pommes de Terre Duchesse
(Rich Mashed Potatoes)

>   2 pounds potatoes, peeled
>   ¼ pound butter
>   4 egg yolks
>   1¼ teaspoons salt
>   ⅛ teaspoon white pepper

Cook the potatoes in boiling salted water until tender; drain and shake over low heat until dry. Mash the potatoes with the butter. Beat in the egg yolks, salt and pepper. Serve as they are, or form into nests and bake in 400° oven until browned. Serves 6-8.

VARIATION:

Croquettes des Pommes de Terre Lyonnaise

Add 1 cup sautéed onions to Pommes de Terre Duchesse. Shape into cylinders 2 inches long and ½ inch wide. Fry in 375° fat until browned.

Gratin des Pommes de Terre
(Potatoes in Cream)

> 5 potatoes (2 pounds)
> 2 teaspoons salt
> ½ teaspoon freshly ground black pepper
> ⅛ teaspoon nutmeg
> 1½ cups light cream
> 2 tablespoons butter

Peel the potatoes and splice paper-thin. In a buttered 9-inch pie plate, make layers of the potatoes, sprinkled with a mixture of the salt, pepper and nutmeg. Pour the cream over all and dot with the butter. Bake in a 300° oven 1 hour, or until tender and browned. Serves 4-6.

Potatoes Yvette

> 1½ pounds potatoes
> 2 tablespoons vegetable oil
> 2 tablespoons butter
> 1¼ teaspoons salt
> ¼ teaspoon white pepper

Peel the potatoes; grate on a long grater into ice water. Soak 10 minutes, then drain and dry on paper towels.

Heat the oil and butter in a 10-inch skillet; add the potatoes, salt and pepper. Shake pan to coat pieces, then cook over low heat until bottom browns. Turn over in 1 piece, then brown other side. Serves 4-6.

Hash-Browned Potatoes

> 3 cups chopped cooked cold potatoes
> 3 tablespoons flour
> ¼ cup milk
> 1½ teaspoons salt
> ¼ teaspoon pepper
> ¼ cup chopped onion
> 3 tablespoons vegetable oil

Mix the potatoes with the flour and milk. Add the salt, pepper and onion; mix well. Heat 2 tablespoons oil in a heavy 9-inch skillet. Add potato mixture and pack with a spoon to cover bottom of pan. Cook over medium heat until brown and crusty. Shake pan occasionally to keep potatoes from sticking. Turn potatoes out onto a flat plate. Wipe pan; heat the remaining tablespoon of oil. Slide potatoes back into pan with brown side up. Cook until bottom is brown. Serves 4-6.

Potato-Green Pea Curry

> 4 tablespoons butter
> 1½ cups thinly sliced onions
> 1 pound potatoes, peeled and sliced
> 1½ teaspoons turmeric
> ¼ teaspoon powdered ginger
> ½ teaspoon freshly ground black pepper
> 3 tomatoes, chopped
> 1 pound green peas, shelled, or 1 package frozen, thawed
> 2 cups boiling water
> 1½ teaspoons salt
> 2 tablespoons lemon juice
> 2 tablespoons minced parsley

Melt the butter in a skillet; sauté the onions 10 minutes. Mix in the potatoes, turmeric, ginger and pepper; sauté 3 minutes, shaking the pan frequently. Add the tomatoes; cook over low heat 10 minutes. Add the peas and water, cover and cook over medium heat 12 minutes. Mix in the salt and lemon juice; cook 1 minute longer. Sprinkle with the parsley. Serves 4-6.

Potato Curry

> 4 tablespoons butter
> 1½ teaspoons turmeric
> 2 pounds potatoes, peeled and quartered

    1 cup boiling water
    1½ teaspoons salt
    ½ teaspoon dried ground red peppers
    2 tablespoons minced parsley

Melt the butter in a skillet; stir in the turmeric, then add the potatoes. Cook over low heat 5 minutes, shaking the pan frequently. Add the water, salt and red peppers; cook over medium heat 10 minutes longer, or until tender. Sprinkle with the parsley. Serves 4-6.

Pommes Bonne Bouche
(Potatoes, Artichokes and Truffles)

    ¼ pound butter
    3 cups cubed potatoes
    1 package frozen artichokes, thawed
    1½ teaspoons salt
    ¼ teaspoon freshly ground black pepper
    3 black truffles, cut julienne

Melt half the butter in a skillet; sauté the potatoes until browned and tender, shaking the pan frequently. Meanwhile, melt the remaining butter in a skillet; sauté the artichokes 6 minutes, shaking the pan frequently. Combine with the potatoes; add the salt, pepper and truffles. Toss together lightly until well mixed. Serves 6-8.

NOTE: The truffles make this an extravagant dish, but it's an exciting presentation. Use more truffles if desired. (Spanish truffles are less expensive than the French or Italian.)

Potato Paprika

    2 pounds potatoes
    4 tablespoons olive oil
    1½ cups chopped onion
    1 clove garlic, minced

1 teaspoon paprika
2 teaspoons salt
½ teaspoon caraway seeds
1 green pepper, cut julienne
2 tomatoes, cubed
2 cups boiling water

Peel the potatoes and cut as for french fries. Heat the oil in a saucepan; sauté the onion 10 minutes. Mix in the garlic, paprika, salt and caraway seeds, then add the potatoes, green pepper and tomatoes. Cook over heat 10 minutes, mixing frequently. Add the water; cover and cook over low heat 25 minutes. Serves 6-8.

NOTE: Slices of sausages or frankfurters may be added with the boiling water, if desired.

Pommes Soufflées

Peel and slice large potatoes into slices ⅛ inch thick. Heat deep fat to 350°. Fry the slices 7 minutes without crowding the pan. Drain and cool. Just before serving, reheat the fat to 375°. Refry the slices until puffed and browned.

A word of caution: not all the slices will puff. Buy old potatoes, for younger potatoes will not puff up properly. This preparation requires practice, so try it several times.

Charcoal-Baked Potato Strips

Peel 1 baking potato for each person. Cut in julienne strips ½ inch thick. Place on a large piece of aluminum foil in a single layer. Season with salt and pepper and dot with 1 tablespoon of butter. Cover with another piece of foil and seal the edges carefully. Place directly on the charcoal. Roast 15 minutes, turning the package once.

Potatoes and Peas in Cream

1 pound small new potatoes
1 package frozen green peas
⅔ cup heavy cream
¼ teaspoon freshly ground black pepper

Peel the potatoes and cook in a small amount of boiling salted water until almost tender. Add peas; continue cooking until vegetables are tender. Drain; add the cream and pepper. Heat. Serves 4-6.

Baked Stuffed Potatoes

6 baking potatoes
3 tablespoons butter
1½ teaspoons salt
⅛ teaspoon freshly ground black pepper
Dash of nutmeg
¼ cup hot milk
1 egg yolk
1 egg white, beaten stiff
6 tablespoons grated Cheddar cheese

Wash and dry the potatoes; prick with a fork. Bake in a 400° oven 1 hour, or until tender. Cut a 1-inch slice off each potato; scoop out the pulp, reserving the shells. Mash potato with the butter, salt, pepper, nutmeg and milk until very fluffy. Beat in the egg yolk, then fold in the white. Stuff the shells; sprinkle with the cheese. Bake in a preheated 350° oven 20 minutes, or until browned. Serves 6.

Pan-Roasted Potatoes

Peel medium potatoes and boil 10 minutes. Drain, arrange around roast of beef or poultry about 1 hour before meat is done. Turn potatoes occasionally and baste with drippings in pan. If potatoes are not browned enough when the roast is finished, brown under the broiler. Sprinkle with salt.

Potato Boats

> 3 cups mashed potatoes
> 1 teaspoon salt
> ⅛ teaspoon freshly ground black pepper
> 2 tablespoons melted butter
> 2 tablespoons minced parsley
> 2 eggs
> 1 cup dry bread crumbs
> Vegetable oil for deep frying

Beat together until light and fluffy the potatoes, salt, pepper, butter, parsley and 1 egg. Chill for 1 hour. Divide into 6 parts and form each into a round cake 1¼ inches thick. Beat the remaining egg and dip the cakes into it, and then into the bread crumbs. Use a 1-inch cooky cutter and press it into the center of each cake to a depth of ¾ inch. Heat the oil to 375° and fry the cakes in it until browned. Drain well. Carefully scoop out the cut portion. Fill centers with peas, creamed spinach, eggs, etc. Serves 6.

Nova Scotian Potatoes

> 4 medium potatoes, peeled and halved
> 4 small parsnips, peeled and quartered
> 2 teaspoons salt
> ⅓ cup hot milk
> 3 tablespoons butter
> ¼ teaspoon white pepper
> 3 tablespoons chopped scallions (green onions)

Cover the potatoes and parsnips with water; add the salt. Cook until tender; drain well.
Mash the vegetables, then beat in the milk, butter

and pepper until fluffy. Mix in the scallions. Taste for seasoning. Serves 4-6.

VARIATION: Form the mixture into patties; dip in flour. Brown in butter, oil or bacon fat.

Potato Pancakes

> 1 pound potatoes, peeled
> 1 egg, beaten
> 1 egg yolk, beaten
> 1 teaspoon salt
> ¼ teaspoon pepper
> 1 tablespoon flour
> 4 tablespoons vegetable oil

Grate the potatoes into a bowl of ice water. Drain very well. Mix with the egg, egg yolk, salt, pepper and flour. Heat the oil in a skillet; drop the mixture into it by the heaping tablespoon. Fry until browned on both sides. Drain. Serves 3-4.

NOTE: If you have an electric blender, cut the potatoes in small pieces. Run in the blender, then drain. Proceed as directed.

Candied Sweet Potatoes

> 1 cup brown sugar
> ¼ cup orange juice
> 3 tablespoons butter
> ½ teaspoon salt
> 2 cloves
> 6 sweet potatoes, cooked, peeled and quartered

Combine the sugar, orange juice, butter, salt and cloves in a saucepan; bring to a boil and cook over low heat 5 minutes. Arrange the potatoes in a shallow baking dish; pour the syrup over them. Bake in a 375° oven 30 minutes, basting a few times. Serves 6-8.

Baked Diced Potatoes

> 8 cups diced potatoes
> ⅓ cup butter
> ¼ cup minced onion
> 1 cup minced celery
> ¼ cup minced parsley
> 2 teaspoons salt
> ¼ teaspoon pepper

Cook the potatoes in boiling water 5 minutes; drain. Mix in the butter, onion, celery, parsley, salt and pepper. Turn into a shallow buttered baking dish. Bake in a 375° oven 30 minutes. Serves 6-8.

Hungarian Potato Stew

> 4 slices bacon, diced
> 4 tablespoons butter
> ½ cup chopped onion
> 1 clove garlic, minced
> 5 potatoes (2 pounds), peeled and sliced thin
> 1 20-ounce can tomatoes, drained
> 1½ teaspoons salt
> ¼ teaspoon freshly ground black pepper
> ⅛ teaspoon marjoram

Half-cook the bacon; drain well. Melt the butter in a saucepan; sauté the onion and garlic 5 minutes. Add the potatoes and bacon; sauté until potatoes are browned. Add the tomatoes, salt, pepper and marjoram. Bring to a boil, cover and cook over low heat 20 minutes. Shake the pan occasionally. Serves 4-6.

Rissole Potatoes

> Vegetable oil for deep frying
> 4 cups cubed cooked cold potatoes
> 3 tablespoons butter

3 tablespoons chopped green pepper
3 tablespoons chopped pimiento

Heat the oil to 375°. Fry the potato cubes until browned and crisp. Drain on paper towels, then place in a heated serving dish. Keep warm.

Melt the butter in a skillet; sauté the green pepper 3 minutes. Add the pimiento; sauté 1 minute. Sprinkle over the potatoes. Serves 4-6.

* * *

The favorite myth of schooldays is that Sir Walter Raleigh brought the potato from the New World to Ireland. But no evidence is available to support this view. In fact, there is a greater likelihood that it was the Spanish who found potatoes in the South American Andes and brought them to Spain. Later, when the Spanish Armada was wrecked off the Irish coast, potatoes were washed ashore. All of which is enough to show that potatoes and their earliest European history are bathed in a confusion of fact and fiction.

What is known, however, is that potatoes were a godsend for the Irish, deeply in need of a crop which grew underground and not readily subject to destruction in times of civil war. It was almost immediately accepted as the staple Irish food. In France, however, its reception was cool, to say the least. Botanists were quick to point out that the potato, like the tomato, belonged to the nightshade family of plants; as the nightshade was renowned for its poisonous qualities, most people were not anxious to experiment with this new vegetable. It had a proponent, however, a gourmet named Antoine Parmentier, who almost single-handed made the potato acceptable to the skeptical French. In his honor, even today, almost all potato dishes are called "à la Parmentier."

* * *

"Gold and silver dresses may be entrusted to a messenger, but not a mushroom, for he will eat it on the way."

Unknown Roman Commentator, 1st century A.D.

Asparagus-Cheese Pudding

> 1½ pounds asparagus, or 2 packages frozen
> 4 slices white bread, toasted and trimmed
> 1 cup (¼ pound) grated Cheddar cheese
> 2 eggs
> 1 teaspoon salt
> ¼ teaspoon freshly ground black pepper
> 2 cups milk, scalded
> 1 tablespoon melted butter

Wash the fresh asparagus thoroughly; cut 2-inch tips off 8 fresh or frozen asparagus stalks. Cut the remaining fresh or frozen asparagus into 1-inch pieces.

Cut the toast into 1-inch squares. In a buttered 6-by-10-inch baking pan, arrange successive layers of toast, asparagus and cheese. Beat the eggs, salt and pepper. Gradually add the hot milk and butter, mixing steadily to prevent curdling. Pour over the layers. Place in a pan of hot water. Bake in a preheated 325° oven 1 hour, or until the custard is set.

10 minutes before the end of baking time, cook the reserved asparagus tips. Drain and arrange on the pudding. Serves 6-8.

Asparagus Rarebit

> 1 tablespoon butter
> 2 cups (½ pound) grated Cheddar cheese
> ½ teaspoon dry mustard

¾ cup beer or milk
1 teaspoon Worcestershire sauce
1 egg
2 pounds asparagus, or 2 packages frozen, cooked
   and drained
Buttered toast

Cook the butter and cheese over low heat until melted. Blend in the mustard, beer or milk, and Worcestershire sauce. Beat the egg in a bowl; gradually add a little of the sauce, stirring steadily to prevent curdling. Return to the saucepan. Cook, stirring steadily, until thickened. Arrange the asparagus on the toast and pour the sauce over all. Serves 6-8.

Green Bean Pie

3 tablespoons butter
1½ cups chopped onion
1 pound ground beef
1 pound fresh, or 1 package frozen green beans,
   cooked and drained
1¾ teaspoons salt
½ teaspoon freshly ground black pepper
½ teaspoon nutmeg
6 eggs, beaten
1 teaspoon sugar
1 tablespoon lemon juice

Melt the butter in a skillet; sauté the onion 10 minutes. Add the meat; cook until no pink remains, stirring frequently to prevent lumps from forming. Mix in beans, 1 teaspoon salt, ¼ teaspoon pepper and ¼ teaspoon nutmeg; cook 2 minutes. Cool 10 minutes.

Beat the eggs with the sugar, lemon juice and remaining spices. Stir into the bean mixture. Turn into a greased 10-inch pie plate. Bake in a preheated 325° oven 45 minutes, or until browned and set. Serve hot or cold. Serves 4-6.

Green Custard

> 1½ pounds turnip or mustard greens
> ¾ cup water
> 4 tablespoons butter
> ½ cup chopped onion
> 4 tablespoons flour
> 1¼ teaspoons salt
> ¼ teaspoon white pepper
> 2 cups light cream
> 5 egg yolks
> 4 egg whites, beaten stiff

Wash the greens thoroughly; remove the stems and tough ribs. Chop the leaves. Combine with the water; bring to a boil, cover and cook over low heat 10 minutes, or until tender. Drain well and chop fine.

Melt the butter in a saucepan; sauté the onion until soft and yellow. Blend in the flour, salt and pepper. Add the cream gradually, stirring steadily to the boiling point; cook over low heat 5 minutes. Beat the egg yolks in a bowl; gradually add the hot sauce, stirring steadily to prevent curdling. Return to saucepan and cook over low heat, stirring steadily until thickened. Do not let boil. Mix in the greens. Taste for seasoning and cool. Fold in the egg whites.

Turn into a buttered 1½-quart ring mold. Set in a shallow pan of hot water. Bake in a preheated 350° oven 40 minutes, or until set. Run a knife around the edge and carefully turn out onto a heated serving dish. The center may be filled with rice, mashed potatoes or sautéed mushrooms. Serves 4-6.

Corn and Carrot Pudding

> 2 tablespoons butter
> ¼ cup minced onion
> 2 tablespoons flour
> 1 teaspoon salt
> ⅛ teaspoon white pepper

1 teaspoon sugar
1 cup milk
1½ cups finely grated carrots
1½ cups cooked or canned whole-kernel corn
¼ cup chopped green pepper
2 eggs, beaten

Melt the butter in a saucepan; sauté the onion 5 minutes. Blend in the flour, salt, pepper and sugar. Gradually add the milk, stirring steadily to the boiling point; cook over low heat 5 minutes. Mix in the carrots, corn and green pepper, then the eggs. Turn into a buttered 1½-quart baking dish. Bake in a preheated 350° oven 45 minutes, or until set. Serves 4-6.

Pain de Carottes
(Carrot Rice Pudding)

6 cups sliced carrots
¾ cup raw rice
1½ teaspoons salt
3 cups boiling water
3 tablespoons melted butter
2 teaspoons sugar
⅛ teaspoon nutmeg
3 eggs, beaten

Cook the carrots, rice and salt in the boiling water 20 minutes, or until tender. Drain; purée in an electric blender, or force through a sieve. Beat in the butter, sugar, nutmeg and eggs. Taste for seasoning. Turn into a buttered baking dish. Set in a pan of hot water; bake in a preheated 300° oven 45 minutes, or until set. Serves 4-6.

Mousse aux Choux-Fleurs
(Cauliflower Mousse)

4-pound head of cauliflower, or 3 packages frozen
3 tablespoons butter
2 tablespoons flour

1½ teaspoons salt
¼ teaspoon white pepper
1 cup milk
5 eggs

Remove the leaves of the fresh cauliflower and wash thoroughly. Cook in boiling salted water 20 minutes, or until tender. Drain. Cook the frozen cauliflower as package directs. Drain. Purée the cauliflower in an electric blender, or force through a sieve.

Melt the butter in a saucepan; blend in the flour, salt and pepper. Add the milk, stirring steadily to the boiling point; cook over low heat 5 minutes. Beat the eggs in a bowl; gradually add the hot sauce, stirring steadily to prevent curdling. Stir in the cauliflower; taste for seasoning.

Turn into a buttered 1½-quart casserole. Place in a shallow pan, in 2 inches of hot water. Bake in a preheated 375° oven 40 minutes, or until browned and set. Serves 6-8.

Baked Corn and Mushroom Custard

2 tablespoons butter
¼ pound mushrooms, sliced
¼ cup minced onion
¼ cup finely chopped celery
1 20-ounce can cream-style corn
1 tablespoon minced parsley
2 tablespoons chopped pimiento
½ teaspoon salt
⅛ teaspoon pepper
1 egg
¼ cup milk
½ cup soft bread crumbs
½ cup grated Cheddar cheese

Melt the butter in a skillet. Add the mushrooms, onion and celery; sauté 10 minutes. Add the corn, parsley, pimiento, salt and pepper. Beat the egg with the milk; add to corn mixture. Turn into a buttered 1-quart baking

dish. Sprinkle with the crumbs and cheese. Bake in a 350°
oven 50 minutes, or until a knife inserted in the center
comes out clean. Serves 4-6.

Baked Eggplant with Cheese Custard

>   ½ cup bread crumbs
>   ½ cup sifted flour
>   1 teaspoon salt
>   2 small eggplant, peeled and sliced
>   1 cup milk
>   ¼ pound butter
>   2 eggs, beaten
>   ¾ pound Mozzarella cheese, grated
>   3 tablespoons grated Parmesan cheese

Combine the bread crumbs, flour and salt on a piece
of waxed paper. Dip the eggplant slices in the milk and
then in the bread crumb mixture, coating the slices well.
Melt half the butter in a skillet. Sauté eggplant in it until
browned on both sides, adding more butter as necessary.

Combine the eggs, Mozzarella and Parmesan cheese.
Place a layer of eggplant on the bottom of a buttered
baking dish. Spread the cheese mixture on it and cover
with remaining eggplant. Bake in a preheated 375° oven
20 minutes. Serves 6-8.

Mushroom Fondue

>   5 tablespoons butter
>   2 pounds mushrooms, sliced thin
>   1½ teaspoons salt
>   ¼ teaspoon white pepper
>   2 tablespoons flour
>   1 cup light cream
>   1 cup grated Swiss cheese

Melt 3 tablespoons butter in a skillet; sauté the mushrooms 5 minutes. Season with ¾ teaspoon salt and the
pepper.

Melt the remaining butter in a saucepan; blend in the flour and remaining salt. Add the cream gradually, stirring steadily to the boiling point. Mix in the mushrooms; cook over low heat 10 minutes; taste for seasoning. Stir in the cheese until melted. Turn into 1-quart baking dish. Bake in a 425° oven 10 minutes, or until delicately browned. Serves 4-6.

Finnish Mushroom Pudding

> 2½ cups bread cubes
> 2 cups milk
> 6 tablespoons butter
> 2 pounds mushrooms, chopped
> 1 cup chopped onion
> 4 egg yolks, beaten
> 1½ teaspoons salt
> ¼ teaspoon white pepper
> 3 tablespoons minced parsley
> 4 egg whites, beaten stiff
> 2 tablespoons dry bread crumbs

Soak the bread in the milk until soft, then mash smooth.

Melt 3 tablespoons butter in a skillet; sauté the mushrooms 5 minutes. Remove. Melt the remaining butter in the skillet; sauté the onion 10 minutes. Mix together the mashed bread, mushrooms, onion, egg yolks, salt, pepper and parsley. Fold in the egg whites. Turn into a buttered 1½-quart baking dish. Sprinkle with the bread crumbs. Put baking dish in a shallow pan of water. Bake in a preheated 350° oven 50 minutes, or until browned and set. Serve immediately. Serves 4-6.

Onion-Cheese Custard

> 2 large Bermuda onions, sliced
> 2 cups bread cubes
> ¾ cup grated Cheddar cheese

¾ cup milk
2 eggs, beaten
¾ teaspoon salt
⅛ teaspoon pepper
2 tablespoons butter

Cook the onion slices in boiling, salted water 10 minutes. Drain slices and place half of them in a shallow buttered baking dish. Scatter half of the bread cubes over the onion slices; cover with half the cheese. Repeat onion, bread cubes, and cheese layers. Beat together the milk, eggs, salt and pepper; pour into the baking dish. Dot with butter. Bake in a 350° oven 40 minutes, or until a knife inserted in the center comes out clean. Serves 4.

Onion-Cheese Pie

3 cups thinly sliced onions
2 tablespoons butter or margarine
2 cups cottage cheese, drained
¼ cup heavy cream
1 teaspoon salt
¼ teaspoon pepper
9-inch baked pie shell

Sauté the onions in the butter until tender; season to taste. Mix the cheese and cream; season with the salt and pepper. Pour into the pie shell; cover with the onions. Bake in a preheated 400° oven 15 minutes. Serves 6-8.

Onion-Nut Soufflé

4 cups chopped white onions
2 cups milk
3 tablespoons butter
4 tablespoons flour
1½ teaspoons salt
½ teaspoon white pepper

    5 egg yolks
    ½ cup chopped walnuts
    2 tablespoons minced parsley
    5 egg whites, beaten stiff

Cook the onions in 1 cup milk 15 minutes, or until tender.

Melt the butter in a saucepan; blend in the flour, salt and pepper. Gradually add the remaining milk, stirring steadily to the boiling point. Cook over low heat 8 minutes. Beat the egg yolks in a bowl; gradually add the hot sauce, stirring steadily to prevent curdling. Mix in the undrained onions, the nuts and parsley. Taste for seasoning. Cool 15 minutes. Fold in the egg whites. Turn into a 1½-quart soufflé dish. Bake in a preheated 350° oven 35 minutes, or until browned and set. Serves 6-8.

Onion Tart

    3 tablespoons butter
    3 cups thinly sliced onions
    2 eggs
    2 cups sour cream
    1½ teaspoons salt
    ¼ teaspoon white pepper
    ⅛ teaspoon nutmeg
    9-inch unbaked pastry shell
    ½ teaspoon paprika
    1 teaspoon caraway seeds (optional)

Melt the butter in a skillet; sauté the onions 15 minutes, or until soft and lightly browned. Beat together the eggs, sour cream, salt, pepper and nutmeg; stir in the onions. Turn into the lined pie plate. Sprinkle with the paprika and caraway. Bake in a preheated 450° oven 10 minutes. Reduce heat to 350° and bake 30 minutes longer, or until a knife inserted in the center comes out clean. Serve hot. Serves 6-8.

Pissaladière
(Provençale Onion Pie)

> ¼ cup olive oil
> 4 tablespoons butter
> 3 cups chopped onions
> 1 teaspoon salt
> ½ teaspoon freshly ground black pepper
> 1 9-inch baked pastry shell
> 2 cans fillets of anchovies
> 1 cup sliced black olives

Heat the oil and butter in a skillet; sauté the onions over very low heat until tender and lightly browned. Season with the salt and pepper. Cool, then spread in the pastry shell. Drain and chop the anchovies. Sprinkle over the onions with the olives. Mix lightly with a fork. Bake in a preheated 375° oven 10 minutes. Serve hot. Serves 6.

Frittata di Spinacio
(Spinach Pancake-Omelet)

> 3 tablespoons olive oil
> ¼ cup minced onion
> 1 clove garlic
> 4 eggs
> 1 teaspoon salt
> ⅛ teaspoon freshly ground black pepper
> ⅛ teaspoon thyme
> ¼ cup grated Parmesan cheese
> 1 cup chopped cooked spinach
> ½ cup dry bread crumbs

Heat 1 tablespoon oil in a skillet; saute' the onion and garlic until soft and yellow. Discard the garlic.

Beat together the eggs, salt, pepper and thyme. Mix in the cheese, spinach, bread crumbs, onion and 1 tablespoon oil. Taste for seasoning.

Wipe the skillet clean of any onion. Heat the remaining oil in the skillet; pour the mixture into it. Cook over low heat until shrunk away from the sides of the pan, then place under a hot broiler to brown the top. Serves 3-4.

Spanakopita
(Greek Spinach Pie)

The pastry used in this dish is extremely thin. Packaged *strudel* leaves or *phyllo* sheets (available in Greek, Armenian or Turkish stores) may be used. You will need 10 sheets. (A very thin pie pastry may be substituted with good, but not perfect results. Prepare in a 9-inch pie plate, using 2 crusts.)

>   2 *pounds spinach, or 2 packages frozen, thawed*
>   2 *teaspoons salt*
>   ½ *teaspoon freshly ground black pepper*
>   ¾ *cup olive oil*
>   1½ *cups chopped scallions (green onions)*
>   2 *tablespoons minced dill*
>   2 *tablespoons minced parsley*
>   ½ *pound feta (Greek) cheese, mashed or ½ pound drained cottage cheese and ¼ cup grated Parmesan cheese*

Wash the fresh spinach, drain and chop it. Sprinkle the fresh or frozen spinach with the salt and ¼ teaspoon pepper; let stand 1 hour. Press all the liquid from it.

Heat ¼ cup oil in a skillet; sauté the scallions 5 minutes. Mix in the spinach; cook over low heat 5 minutes, stirring frequently. Transfer to a bowl; mix in the dill, parsley, cheese and remaining pepper.

Brush an 8-by-12-inch shallow baking pan with oil. Line it with 1 sheet of pastry. Brush pastry with oil and cover with 4 more sheets, brushing each with oil. Spread spinach mixture over it and cover with remaining 5 sheets, brushing each with oil. With a knife, score the top into squares and brush lightly with cold water. Bake in a preheated 350° oven 40 minutes, or until browned.

Cool 10 minutes before cutting through the squares.
Serves 6-8.

Zucchini in Custard Sauce

> 4 zucchini (2 pounds)
> 4 tablespoons butter
> 1¼ cups heavy cream
> 1½ teaspoons salt
> ¼ teaspoon freshly ground black pepper
> 2 egg yolks

Wash the zucchini and scrape lightly; slice ½ inch
thick. Cook in boiling salted water 5 minutes. Drain well.
Melt the butter in a saucepan; add the zucchini and toss
until coated. Mix in 1 cup cream, the salt and pepper;
cook over low heat 10 minutes, or until tender.

Beat the egg yolks and remaining cream in a bowl; add
a little hot liquid, stirring steadily to prevent curdling.
Mix into the zucchini. Heat, stirring steadily, but do not
let boil. Serves 4-6.

* * *

Spinach has always had to fight a losing battle with
adults, after a childhood in which most of us were given
the worst possible introduction to a vegetable: "Eat your
spinach; it's good for you!" Most of us have recovered
from this standardized, almost obligatory, childhood
trauma, and can enjoy spinach for its fresh, garden flavor.

Earliest records? Spinach was first noted in Asia Minor,
probably in the vicinity of what was then called Persia.
Its peregrinations brought the leafy plant westward into
France and Spain, where it was well received. The theory
has even been advanced that the word spinach comes
from the word Spanish, for the Iberians became staunch
advocates of the leafy green. Medieval writings are filled
with references to "spynoches," "spinoches," and even
"spanitches." It was first brought to the United States
towards the end of the 18th century.

Dumplings, Fritters, Pancakes, Noodles and Stuffings

Browned Cabbage and Noodles, Hungarian Style

  3-pound cabbage
  1 tablespoon salt
  1½ sticks (⅜ pound) butter
  3 tablespoons grated onion
  2 teaspoons sugar
  ½ teaspoon freshly ground black pepper
  1 pound broad noodles, cooked and drained

Wash the cabbage and grate or shred very fine. Mix in the salt and let stand 2 hours. Rinse, drain and dry.

Melt half the butter in a deep large skillet or Dutch oven. Mix in the cabbage, onion, sugar and pepper. Cook over low heat 1¼ hours, stirring frequently. Add the remaining butter after 1 hour. Toss in the noodles until thoroughly mixed with the cabbage. Taste for seasoning and cook over low heat 5 minutes. Serves 6-8.

Corn Fritters

  1 egg, beaten
  ½ cup milk
  2 cups corn kernels
  1½ cups sifted flour
  2 teaspoons baking powder
  1 teaspoon salt
  ¼ teaspoon pepper

1 tablespoon melted butter
Vegetable oil for deep frying

Combine the egg, milk and corn. Sift together the flour, baking powder and salt; add to corn mixture and beat well. Stir in pepper and melted butter. Heat the fat to 375°. Drop the batter into it by the tablespoon and fry until golden brown. Drain on absorbent paper. Serves 4-6.

Corn Pancakes

2 cups cream-style corn
2 tablespoons flour
1 teaspoon baking powder
1 teaspoon sugar
¾ teaspoon salt
⅛ teaspoon pepper
1 tablespoon melted butter or margarine
1 tablespoon heavy cream
2 egg yolks, beaten
2 egg whites, beaten stiff

Combine the corn, flour, baking powder, sugar, salt, pepper, butter and cream. Stir in the yolks, then fold in the whites. If too thin, add a little more flour. Drop by spoonfuls onto hot, greased griddle; turn to brown both sides. Makes about 4 dozen 3-inch cakes.

Beignets de Mais
(Corn Puffs)

1 cup milk
1 teaspoon salt
⅛ teaspoon cayenne pepper
4 tablespoons butter
1 cup flour
4 eggs
1 cup cooked or canned corn kernels
Vegetable oil for deep frying

Combine and bring to a boil the milk, salt, cayenne
pepper and butter. When butter melts, mix in the flour
all at once. Cook over low heat, stirring steadily, until
mixture leaves the sides of the pan. Remove from heat.
Add 1 egg at a time, beating well after each addition.
Beat in the corn.

Heat the fat to 375°. Drop the batter into it by the
tablespoon. Fry 5 minutes, or until browned. Makes
about 16.

Fritto Misto

Any combination of ingredients can be used in a fritto
misto—green beans, cauliflower flowerets, mushrooms,
sliced artichokes, sliced eggplant, sliced zucchini. Have
everything cut in bite-sized pieces; sprinkle with salt and
pepper, then dip in the batter. Fry in deep 370° fat until
browned. Drain and heap on a serving dish. Sprinkle
with parsley and garnish with lemon wedges.

Batter:

> 1½ cups sifted flour
> ¼ teaspoon salt
> 5 tablespoons oil
> 1 cup lukewarm water
> 2 egg whites, beaten stiff
> Fat for deep frying

Sift the flour and salt into a bowl. Stir in the oil, then
gradually mix in the water until creamy and smooth. Set
aside for 2 hours. Just before using, fold in the egg
whites. Makes enough batter for 8 portions.

Potato-Cheese Fritters

> 2 cups seasoned mashed potatoes
> 2 egg yolks
> ⅓ cup grated Parmesan cheese
> 2 tablespoons minced parsley
> 2 egg whites, beaten stiff
> Vegetable oil for deep frying

Beat together the potatoes, egg yolks, Parmesan cheese and parsley; fold in the egg whites.

Heat the oil to 370°; drop the mixture into it by the tablespoon. Fry until browned. Drain well. Makes about 24.

Potato Dumplings

2½ pounds potatoes
½ cup minced onion
3 tablespoons butter
1 teaspoon salt
⅛ teaspoon white pepper
2 eggs, beaten
1 cup sifted flour
4 slices crisp bacon, crumbled (optional)

Cook the unpeeled potatoes until tender. Peel and put through a ricer, or mash very smooth. Sauté the onion in the butter until soft and yellow. Beat into the potatoes with the salt, pepper, eggs, flour and bacon. Shape tablespoons of the mixture into balls. Cook in boiling salted water 5 minutes, or until they rise to the surface. Drain well. Don't cook too many at once. Serve with browned butter. Serves 6-8.

Onion Stuffing

¼ pound butter
3 cups chopped onions
½ cup chopped celery
½ cup chopped parsley
2 cups hot water
5 cups soft bread crumbs
2 eggs, beaten
1½ teaspoons salt
½ teaspoon freshly ground black pepper
2 teaspoons poultry seasoning
2 teaspoons sage or thyme (optional)

Melt the butter in a skillet; sauté the onions 10 minutes, stirring frequently. Mix in the celery and parsley. Pour the hot water over the bread crumbs; cool 5 minutes. Mix in the eggs, salt, pepper, poultry seasoning, sage or thyme and the sautéed vegetables. Makes enough for a 10-pound turkey, 2 chickens, a suckling pig or a crown roast of pork or lamb.

Sweet Potato Stuffing

> 6 cups mashed sweet potatoes (about 8 potatoes)
> 1¼ cups unstrained orange juice
> ½ cup melted butter
> 2 tablespoons grated orange rind
> ¼ cup dry sherry

Mix all the ingredients together lightly. Taste for seasoning. Makes enough for a 6-pound chicken, a duck, or a crown roast of pork.

Grated Potato Stuffing

> 2 pounds potatoes, peeled, grated and drained
> ¼ cup grated onion
> ½ cup sifted flour
> 2 eggs, beaten
> 1½ teaspoons salt
> ¼ teaspoon white pepper
> ¼ cup chopped parsley
> ¼ cup melted butter or chicken fat

Mix all the ingredients together. Makes enough for a 5-pound chicken, or a breast of veal.

Risi e Bisi
(Rice and Peas)

> 2 tablespoons olive oil
> 4 tablespoons butter
> ½ cup chopped onion

1 cup raw rice
2 tablespoons dry sherry
2 cups shelled peas, or 1 package frozen, thawed
2 cups hot chicken broth
1¼ teaspoons salt
¼ teaspoon white pepper
¼ cup grated Parmesan cheese

Heat the oil and 2 tablespoons butter in a heavy saucepan; sauté the onion 5 minutes. Mix in the rice until translucent. Add the sherry; cook over low heat 1 minute. Add the peas, broth, salt and pepper. Cover, bring to a boil and cook over low heat 15 minutes, or until rice is tender. Taste for seasoning; mix in the cheese and remaining butter. Serves 4-6.

Spinach-Cheese Dumplings

1 pound ricotta or cottage cheese
2 pounds spinach, or 2 packages frozen, thawed
5 egg yolks
3 cups freshly grated Parmesan cheese
⅛ teaspoon nutmeg
¾ cup flour
½ cup melted butter

Press all the liquid from the ricotta or cottage cheese
—it must be very dry.

Bring the spinach to a boil in salted water and drain thoroughly at once. Purée in an electric blender, or chop very fine. Drain again if necessary.

Beat the egg yolks, then mix in the drained ricotta or cottage cheese, spinach, 2 cups Parmesan cheese and the nutmeg. Beat well with a wooden spoon. Shape into balls and roll lightly in the flour.

Use a large deep skillet and almost fill it with water. Bring to a boil and reduce heat to low. Carefully add the dumplings one at a time. Cook over low heat until they rise to the surface. Drain well. Pour the melted butter over them and sprinkle with the remaining Parmesan cheese. Serves 6-8.

Lo Mein
(Vegetables and Noodles)

>   1 raw chicken breast
>   4 tablespoons vegetable oil
>   1 cup thinly sliced onions
>   1 cup sliced celery
>   2 cups shredded Chinese or green cabbage
>   2 cups bean sprouts, fresh or canned
>   1 teaspoon salt
>   ¼ teaspoon freshly ground black pepper
>   3 tablespoons soy sauce
>   1 teaspoon sugar
>   2 tablespoons cornstarch
>   1¼ cups chicken broth
>   2 cups cooked, drained fine noodles

Remove the skin and bones of the chicken; cut in julienne pieces. Heat the oil in a skillet; sauté the chicken 5 minutes. Mix in the onions, celery, cabbage, bean sprouts, salt, pepper, soy sauce and sugar. Cover and cook over low heat 3 minutes. Mix the cornstarch and broth together until smooth. Add to the skillet, stirring constantly until thickened. Add the noodles; cook 3 minutes, stirring frequently. Serves 3-4.

*　　*　　*

The mushroom is a fungus, not a true vegetable, although it is so considered by most people. Botanists, indifferent to popular beliefs and fancies, call the mushroom the "fruiting body of an edible fungus." The Egyptians were the first to proclaim the marvels of mushrooms, often associating them with divinity. Folklore, notably that of Central Europe, is replete with references to mushrooms and the little people that inhabited them. During the reign of Louis XIV, mushroom culture began on a large scale in the *faubourgs,* or suburbs of Paris. A few decades later, this first attempt at mass production had proved so successful that there were well over a thousand miles of mushroom beds in these suburban caves.

Stuffed Vegetables

Stuffed Artichokes

> 6 artichokes
> 1 cup soft bread crumbs
> ½ cup finely chopped onion
> 3 tablespoons minced parsley
> 6 anchovy fillets, minced
> 2 tablespoons chopped capers
> 4 tablespoons olive oil
> 1 cup chicken broth

Buy medium-sized artichokes; wash and soak in cold water, stem up, for 30 minutes. Drain well; cut off the stem and force the leaves open. Cut out the choke (the hairy-looking center). Mix together the bread crumbs, onion, parsley, anchovies, capers and 2 tablespoons oil. Fill the centers and brush with the remaining oil. Arrange in a buttered baking dish; add the broth. Bake in a 350° oven 1 hour, basting frequently. Serve hot or cold. Serves 6.

Cabbage Dolma

> 1 large head of cabbage
> ½ cup yellow split peas
> 1 pound ground beef
> ¾ cup chopped onion
> ¼ cup chopped parsley
> ½ teaspoon cinnamon
> 2 teaspoons salt
> ½ teaspoon freshly ground black pepper
> 1½ cups water

½ cup lemon juice
¼ cup sugar

Wash the cabbage, cover with water, bring to a boil and cook over low heat 15 minutes. Drain and carefully remove 24 leaves. (The rest of the cabbage will be used for lining pan and to put between the layers.) Cook the peas in boiling water 30 minutes, or until tender. Drain.

Mix together the peas, beef, onion, parsley, cinnamon, 1 teaspoon salt and ¼ teaspoon pepper. Put a heaping tablespoon of the mixture on each leaf. Fold in the opposite ends, then roll up into sausage shapes. If there is any filling left, use a few more cabbage leaves.

Line the bottom of a deep skillet with cabbage leaves and arrange the rolls in it in layers, placing more leaves between the layers. Add the water and the remaining salt, pepper and cabbage. Cover and cook over low heat 30 minutes. Mix in the lemon juice and sugar. Cook 30 minutes longer; taste for seasoning. Serves 6-8.

Sweet and Sour Stuffed Cabbage

1 large head of cabbage
2 tablespoons vegetable oil
1 cup sliced onions
1 20-ounce can tomatoes
Beef bones
3 teaspoons salt
½ teaspoon freshly ground black pepper
1½ pounds ground beef
½ cup finely chopped onion
2 eggs
½ cup half-cooked rice
¼ cup cold water
4 tablespoons brown sugar
3 tablespoons lemon juice
¼ cup seedless raisins (optional)

Place the cabbage in boiling water and let stand 15 minutes to soften. Remove 18 leaves carefully. Shred 2 cups cabbage.

Heat the oil in a Dutch oven or heavy saucepan; sauté the sliced onions 10 minutes. Mix in the shredded cabbage, then add the tomatoes, bones and half the salt and pepper. Cook over low heat 30 minutes.

Prepare the cabbage rolls meanwhile by mixing the beef, chopped onion, eggs, rice, water and remaining salt and pepper. Place a heaping tablespoon on each cabbage leaf. Turn opposite ends in and roll up. Arrange in the pan. Cover and cook over low heat 1¼ hours. Add the brown sugar, lemon juice and raisins. Cover again and cook 30 minutes longer. Taste for seasoning. Serves 6-9.

Mushroom-Stuffed Cabbage

>   1 head of cabbage
>   3 tablespoons vegetable oil
>   ½ pound mushrooms, sliced
>   ½ cup chopped onion
>   ½ cup raw rice
>   1 cup boiling water
>   1½ teaspoons salt
>   ¼ teaspoon freshly ground black pepper
>   1 cup canned tomato sauce

Cover the cabbage with boiling water and let stand 10 minutes to soften. Carefully remove 16 leaves.

Heat 1 tablespoon of the oil in a skillet; sauté the mushrooms and onion 10 minutes. Heat 1 tablespoon oil in a saucepan; stir the rice into it until yellow. Add the water; cover and cook over low heat until tender and dry. Mix in the sautéed vegetables, salt and pepper. Place a heaping tablespoon of the mixture on each cabbage leaf; turn in the ends and roll up.

Shred half the remaining cabbage and spread in a casserole; arrange the cabbage rolls over it. Add the tomato sauce and remaining oil. Cover and bake in a 350° oven 1 hour, removing the cover for the last 15 minutes. Taste for seasoning. Serves 4 as a main course; 8 as a vegetable.

〜〜〜〜〜〜〜〜〜〜〜〜〜〜〜〜〜〜〜〜〜〜〜〜

Repollo en Sorpreso
(Stuffed Cabbage, Spanish Style)

> 4-pound solid head of cabbage
> ½ pound sausage meat
> 1 cup cooked rice
> 1 cup chopped cooked spinach
> ½ cup chopped onion
> 2 cloves garlic, minced
> 1 tomato, chopped
> 1 teaspoon salt
> ¼ teaspoon freshly ground black pepper
> 4 cups beef broth

Wash the cabbage thoroughly. Cut off the stem end, and then scoop out the center of the top. Chop the scooped-out portion; mix with the sausage meat, rice, spinach, onion, garlic, tomato, salt and pepper. Stuff the cabbage, using all the mixture. Tie in cheesecloth. Place in a saucepan with the broth; bring to a boil, cover and cook over low heat 2 hours. Add a little more broth or boiling water while cooking to keep liquid almost to the top of the cabbage. Lift out, drain well and unwrap. Cut in wedges. Serves 4-6.

Golombki
(Polish Stuffed Cabbage)

> 1 large head of cabbage
> ½ pound ground beef
> ½ pound ground veal
> ½ pound ground pork
> 1 cup half-cooked rice
> 2½ teaspoons salt
> ½ teaspoon freshly ground black pepper
> 1 egg
> 2 cups beef broth
> 1 8-ounce can tomato sauce
> ¾ cup seedless raisins
> ½ cup sour cream

Wash the cabbage thoroughly. Cover with water, bring to a boil and cook over low heat 5 minutes. Drain. Cool and carefully remove 18-20 outer leaves.

Mix together the meats, rice, 1½ teaspoons salt, ¼ teaspoon pepper and the egg. Place a tablespoon of the mixture on each leaf, tuck the ends in and roll up. (If there is meat mixture left, use more cabbage leaves, or make meat balls which can be put in the dish.) Arrange the rolls in a baking dish. Mix together the broth, tomato sauce and remaining salt and pepper. Pour over the rolls. Cover dish, bake in a 300° oven 1 hour. Add raisins; bake, uncovered, 45 minutes longer. Mix in the sour cream and taste for seasoning. Serves 6-8.

Stuffed Grape Leaves

> 1 can grape leaves
> 2 cups beef broth
> ¼ cup lemon juice
> 1 tablespoon tomato paste

Buy the grape leaves in Greek, Armenian or specialty shops. Use 40 leaves for stuffing, and the rest for lining the pan and between the layers. Drain the leaves and cover with hot water. Drain and spread out on a flat surface. Cut off the stems. Put a tablespoon of the selected filling (below) on each leaf. Fold opposite ends toward the center, then roll up like a sausage. Cover the bottom of a heavy deep skillet with leaves and arrange the rolls in layers, separating each layer with leaves. Add a mixture of the broth, lemon juice and tomato paste. Put a plate on top to weight it down, and cover the skillet. Cook over low heat 1¼ hours, or until tender.

Rice Filling (For Grape Leaves)

> ¾ cup olive oil
> 3 cups chopped onions
> 1¼ cups raw rice
> ¼ cup currants or seedless raisins

¾ cup chopped dill or parsley
1¼ teaspoons salt
½ teaspoon freshly ground black pepper
½ teaspoon ground allspice
½ cup boiling water

Heat ½ cup oil in a skillet; mix in the onions and rice. Sauté over low heat 15 minutes, stirring very frequently. Mix in the currants, dill, salt, pepper and allspice; cook 3 minutes. Add the remaining oil and water. Cover and cook over very low heat 20 minutes, or until tender. Watch carefully to prevent burning. Proceed as directed in recipe for Stuffed Grape Leaves. Serve hot or cold. Garnish with lemon slices. Serves 6-8.

Meat Stuffing (For Grape Leaves)

1 pound ground beef
1 cup half-cooked rice
1½ teaspoons salt
½ teaspoon freshly ground black pepper
½ teaspoon cinnamon
½ cup chopped scallions (green onions)
½ cup chopped parsley
2 tablespoons melted butter

Mix all the ingredients together lightly. Proceed as directed in recipe for Stuffed Grape Leaves. Serve hot, with yogurt. Serves 6-8.

Stuffed Kohlrabi

8 kohlrabi
½ cup chopped onion
¾ pound sausage meat
½ cup bread cubes
1 egg, beaten
1 hard-cooked egg, chopped
¼ teaspoon freshly ground black pepper
⅛ teaspoon marjoram

Peel the kohlrabi and cook in boiling salted water 15 minutes, or until tender. Drain. Scoop out the centers and chop fine.

Fry the onion and sausage meat until no pink remains. Mix frequently to prevent lumps from forming. Drain, reserving the fat.

Soak the bread cubes in water 5 minutes. Drain well; mix with the sausage and add the beaten egg, chopped egg, pepper and marjoram. Mix well and taste for seasoning. Stuff the kohlrabi; you will not use all the mixture. Spread the remaining sausage mixture on the bottom of a pie plate. Arrange the kohlrabi over it and brush with the sausage fat. Bake in a preheated 425° oven 15 minutes, basting once or twice with the fat. Serves 4.

NOTE: Chopped beef may be substituted for the sausage meat, if desired.

Baked Stuffed Mushrooms

> 24 large mushrooms
> 4 tablespoons vegetable oil
> ½ cup chopped onion
> ¼ cup chopped green pepper
> ¾ teaspoon salt
> ¼ teaspoon freshly ground black pepper
> 3 tablespoons grated Parmesan cheese
> 1 tablespoon bread crumbs

Wash and dry the mushrooms. Remove the stems and chop fine. Heat 2 tablespoons oil in a skillet; sauté the onion and green pepper 5 minutes. Add the chopped stems; sauté 5 minutes. Mix in the salt, pepper, cheese and bread crumbs; stuff the mushrooms with the mixture. Place in an oiled baking dish and sprinkle with the remaining oil. Bake in a 375° oven 15 minutes. Serves 6.

Funghi alla Parmigiana
(Cheese-Stuffed Mushrooms)

> 1½ pounds mushrooms
> ⅓ cup grated Parmesan cheese

~~~~~~

> *1 cup dry bread crumbs*
> *¼ cup grated onion*
> *2 cloves garlic, minced*
> *2 tablespoons minced parsley*
> *½ teaspoon salt*
> *¼ teaspoon freshly ground black pepper*
> *½ teaspoon oregano*
> *⅔ cup olive oil*

Buy large, even-sized mushrooms. Wash but do not peel them. Remove the stems and chop; mix with the cheese, bread crumbs, onion, garlic, parsley, salt, pepper and oregano. Stuff the mushroom caps with the mixture.

Pour a little oil into a baking pan. Arrange the mushrooms in it. Pour the remaining oil over them, being sure to get a little in each mushroom. Bake in a 350° oven 25 minutes. Serve as an appetizer or as a vegetable. Serves 6-8.

Baked Mushroom-Stuffed Tomatoes

> *4 firm tomatoes*
> *4 tablespoons butter or margarine*
> *½ cup chopped onion*
> *1 cup chopped mushrooms*
> *1 teaspoon salt*
> *¼ teaspoon freshly ground black pepper*
> *¼ teaspoon marjoram*
> *2 cups soft bread crumbs*
> *1 10½-ounce can mushroom soup*

Cut a slice off the stem end of the tomatoes. Scoop out the pulp and reserve. Melt the butter in a skillet; sauté the onion 3 minutes. Add the mushrooms and sauté 3 minutes. Mix in the tomato pulp, salt, pepper and marjoram; cook over low heat 10 minutes. Stir in the bread crumbs. Stuff the tomatoes and arrange in a shallow baking dish; pour the soup around them. Bake in a preheated 375° oven 30 minutes, or until tender. Serves 4.

Stuffed Pepper Salad

> 6 green peppers
> ½ cup olive oil
> 2 tablespoons wine vinegar
> 1 teaspoon salt
> ¼ teaspoon pepper
> ½ teaspoon dry mustard
> ¼ pound American cheese, diced
> ¼ pound Swiss cheese, diced

Place the green peppers in a saucepan with water to cover. Boil 5 minutes. Drain, cool, and cut in half, removing the seeds and fibers. Chill.

Beat together the oil, vinegar, salt, pepper and mustard. Add the American and Swiss cheeses. Marinate for 30 minutes. Stuff the pepper halves with the cheese mixture. Serve on lettuce leaves. Serves 12.

Baked Stuffed Peppers

> 8 large green peppers
> 1 pound ground beef
> ½ cup light cream
> ½ cup soft bread crumbs
> 1 egg, beaten
> ½ cup coarsely chopped nuts
> ¼ teaspoon thyme
> ¼ teaspoon freshly ground black pepper
> 2 teaspoons salt
> 2 8-ounce cans tomato sauce
> ½ cup water

Cut a 1-inch piece from the stem end of the peppers; scoop out the seeds and fibers. Wash and dry.

Mix together the beef, cream, bread crumbs, egg, nuts, thyme, pepper and 1 teaspoon salt. Stuff the peppers; arrange in a baking dish. Mix together the tomato sauce, water and remaining salt; pour over the peppers. Cover tightly; bake in a preheated 400° oven 1 hour, or until peppers are tender. Serves 4-8.

Greek Rice-Stuffed Tomatoes

    8 large firm tomatoes
    2 teaspoons salt
    ½ teaspoon freshly ground black pepper
    ¾ cup olive oil
    1 cup chopped onion
    ½ cup raw rice
    2 tablespoons currants or seedless raisins
    1 cup boiling water
    2 tablespoons minced parsley
    ¼ cup pine nuts or sliced almonds
    ½ cup dry bread crumbs

Cut a ½-inch piece off the stem end of the tomatoes;
reserve tops. Scoop out as much of the pulp as possible.
Sprinkle the insides of the tomatoes with half the salt and
pepper; chop the pulp.

Heat ½ cup oil in a saucepan; brown the onion in it.
Stir in the rice until coated. Mix in the tomato pulp, currants and remaining salt and pepper. Add the water;
cover and cook over low heat 10 minutes. Mix in parsley
and nuts; taste for seasoning. Stuff the tomatoes loosely;
replace the tops. Arrange in an oiled baking dish. Brush
with the remaining oil; sprinkle with the bread crumbs.
Bake in a 350° oven 45 minutes. In Greece, the tomatoes
are usually served cold, but they're delicious hot, too.
Serves 4 as a main course; 8 as a vegetable.

Zucchini Ripieni alla Siciliana
(Stuffed Zucchini, Sicilian Style)

    4 medium-sized zucchini
    ½ cup olive oil
    ¾ cup chopped onion
    1 clove garlic, minced
    ¾ cup peeled chopped tomatoes
    ½ cup chopped mushrooms
    ½ cup fine dry bread crumbs

2 tablespoons minced parsley
2 tablespoons chopped capers
6 anchovies, chopped
1 teaspoon salt
½ teaspoon freshly ground black pepper
¼ teaspoon basil

Scrub the zucchini, but do not peel. Cover with water,
bring to a boil and cook over low heat 3 minutes. Drain,
cool, and cut in half lengthwise. Scoop out the pulp and
dice it. Reserve the shells.

Heat ¼ cup oil in a skillet; sauté the onion 5 minutes.
Add the pulp and garlic; sauté 3 minutes. Mix in the
tomatoes and mushrooms; cook 5 minutes.

Remove from the heat and mix in the bread crumbs,
parsley, capers, anchovies, salt, pepper and basil. Stuff
the shells and place in an oiled baking dish. Sprinkle
with the remaining oil. Bake in a 350° oven 30 minutes.
Serve hot or cold. Serves 4-8.

Baked Stuffed Zucchini

3 medium-sized zucchini (1½ pounds)
3 tablespoons vegetable oil
½ cup chopped onion
1 clove garlic, minced
1¼ teaspoons salt
¼ teaspoon pepper
½ teaspoon oregano
2 cups soft bread crumbs

Wash and scrub the zucchini. Cook in boiling salted
water 8 minutes. Drain well and cut in half lengthwise.
Scoop out the pulp and chop; reserve the shells. Heat
the oil in a skillet; sauté the onion and garlic 5 minutes.
Add the pulp; sauté 5 minutes. Mix in the salt, pepper,
oregano and bread crumbs. Stuff the zucchini; arrange
in a greased baking dish. Bake in a 375° oven 20 minutes,
or until browned and tender. Serves 6.

Basic Rule for Preparing Canned Vegetables

Drain the vegetables. Cook only the liquid until reduced to one-half its original volume. Add the vegetables and season as you like. Heat, drain and serve.

Canned Green Beans, Provençale

> ¼ cup olive oil
> ¾ cup thinly sliced onions
> ½ cup julienne-cut green pepper
> ½ cup chopped celery
> 1 clove garlic, minced
> 1 cup canned tomatoes
> 1 teaspoon salt
> ¼ teaspoon freshly ground black pepper
> 1 bay leaf
> ½ teaspoon oregano
> ¼ cup water
> 1 #2½-can green beans, drained

Heat the oil in a saucepan; sauté the onions 5 minutes. Add the green pepper, celery, garlic, tomatoes, salt, pepper, bay leaf, oregano and water. Bring to a boil and cook over low heat 10 minutes. Add the beans and cook 5 minutes. Taste for seasoning. Serves 4-6.

Lima Beans, New Orleans Style

> 3 slices bacon
> ¾ cup chopped onion
> ½ cup chopped green peppers

1 16-ounce can tomatoes
1 teaspoon sugar
¼ teaspoon basil
1 16-ounce can lima beans, drained
¼ teaspoon freshly ground black pepper

Brown the bacon and remove. Pour off half the fat. In the fat remaining, sauté the onion and green peppers 10 minutes. Add the tomatoes, sugar and basil; bring to a boil, and cook over low heat 20 minutes. Add the beans, pepper and salt to taste. Cook 10 minutes. Crumble the bacon on top. Serves 4.

Old-Fashioned Beans and Corn

4 slices bacon
½ cup chopped onion
1 15½-ounce can cut green beans
1 16-ounce can whole kernel corn, drained
1 tablespoon sugar
¼ cup cider vinegar
¾ teaspoon salt
¼ teaspoon freshly ground black pepper

Fry the bacon crisp; remove and crumble. Pour off all but 2 tablespoons fat; sauté the onion in the fat 5 minutes. Drain the beans; add the liquid to the onion. Cook over high heat until reduced to about ⅓ cup. Add the beans, corn, sugar, vinegar, salt, pepper and bacon; cook over low heat 10 minutes. Serves 6-8.

Baked Bean Casserole

2 tablespoons vegetable oil
1½ cups thinly sliced onions
1½ cups thinly sliced green peppers
2 1-pound cans baked beans
2 cups chopped tomatoes
1 teaspoon salt
½ teaspoon freshly ground black pepper

Heat the oil in a skillet; sauté the onions and green peppers 10 minutes. In a casserole, arrange successive layers of the beans, tomatoes and sautéed vegetables, sprinkling the vegetables with salt and pepper. Finish with a tomato layer. Bake in a 350° oven 30 minutes. Serves 4-6.

Canned Beets in Wine

>   3 tablespoons butter
>   3 tablespoons honey
>   ¼ cup dry sherry
>   ¼ teaspoon nutmeg
>   1 teaspoon grated orange rind
>   1 1-pound can tiny beets, drained

Heat the butter, honey, sherry, nutmeg and orange rind in the top of a double boiler. Add the beets, place over hot water and cook 10 minutes. Taste for seasoning. Serves 4.

Canned Spiced Beets

>   1 16-ounce can sliced beets
>   2 tablespoons butter
>   1 tablespoon olive oil
>   1 tablespoon lemon juice
>   ½ teaspoon salt
>   ¼ teaspoon freshly ground black pepper
>   ½ teaspoon ground coriander
>   3 tablespoons minced parsley

Heat the beets in their liquid, then drain well. Add the butter and olive oil; toss until coated. Sprinkle with the lemon juice, salt, pepper, coriander and parsley. Serves 4-5.

Beets in Orange Sauce

>   4 tablespoons butter
>   ⅓ cup honey

½ cup orange juice
½ teaspoon ground cloves
1 teaspoon grated orange rind
2 1-pound cans tiny beets, drained

Combine all the ingredients in the top of a double boiler; bring to a boil. Place over hot water and let stand 15 minutes before serving. Serves 6-8.

Harvard Beets

2 1-pound cans sliced beets
2 tablespoons cornstarch
½ cup sugar
1 teaspoon salt
½ cup cider vinegar
2 tablespoons butter

Drain the beets, reserving 1 cup liquid. In a saucepan, mix together the cornstarch, sugar, salt and vinegar, then stir in the reserved liquid. Cook over low heat, stirring steadily to the boiling point. Add the beets and butter; cook 10 minutes. Serves 6-8.

Marinated Canned Carrots

1 16-ounce can carrots
¼ cup olive oil
2 tablespoons wine vinegar
2 cloves garlic, minced
¾ teaspoon salt
¼ teaspoon freshly ground black pepper
½ teaspoon oregano

Drain the carrots and place in a dish. Mix together the oil, vinegar, garlic, salt, pepper and oregano. Pour over the carrots; marinate in the refrigerator at least 4 hours before serving. Serves 3-4.

Chicken Divan

>   3 packages boil-in-a-bag broccoli au gratin
>   16 slices cooked chicken or turkey
>   1 teaspoon salt
>   ¼ teaspoon freshly ground black pepper
>   ⅓ cup light cream
>   3 tablespoons grated Parmesan cheese

Place the bags of broccoli in boiling water; cook 8 minutes. Open the bags, and place the contents of 1½ bags in a buttered baking dish. Arrange the chicken or turkey over it; sprinkle with the salt and pepper. Mix the remaining broccoli with the cream; pour over the chicken or turkey. Sprinkle with the cheese. Bake in a preheated 400° oven 20 minutes. Serves 4-6.

Corn and Peas

>   1 12-ounce can corn kernels
>   1 16-ounce can green peas
>   ½ teaspoon marjoram
>   2 tablespoons minced parsley
>   2 tablespoons butter
>   ¼ teaspoon freshly ground black pepper

Drain the corn and peas, but reserve ½ cup of the green pea liquid. Cook the liquid over high heat until reduced to ¼ cup. Add the vegetables, marjoram, parsley, butter and pepper. Heat and taste for seasoning. Serves 4-6.

Canned Peas and Cheese

>   ½ cup chopped onion
>   4 tablespoons butter
>   1 16-ounce can peas, heated and drained
>   3 tablespoons minced parsley

    ⅛ teaspoon freshly ground black pepper
    3 tablespoons grated Parmesan cheese

Sauté the onions in the butter until tender and browned. Toss with the peas, parsley, pepper, cheese and add salt to taste. Serves 3-4.

Quick Purée of Peas

    1 16-ounce can green peas
    ½ cup light cream
    3 tablespoons butter
    ½ teaspoon salt
    ⅛ teaspoon white pepper
    ⅛ teaspoon mace

Drain the peas; combine in an electric blender with the remaining ingredients and run until smooth. Or force the peas through a food mill, then mix with remaining ingredients. Cook over low heat until hot, stirring almost constantly. Serves 2-4.

Quick Spinach Soufflé

    3 packages boil-in-a-bag creamed spinach
    4 egg yolks, beaten
    1 teaspoon salt
    ¼ teaspoon white pepper
    ⅛ teaspoon nutmeg
    1 tablespoon cognac
    4 egg whites, beaten stiff

Heat the spinach by boiling bags in water 8 minutes. Empty bags into a bowl. Mix in the egg yolks, salt, pepper, nutmeg and cognac. Cool 10 minutes. Fold in the egg whites. Turn into a 1½-quart soufflé dish. Bake in a preheated 350° oven 30 minutes, or until set and browned. Serves 4-6.

Mixed Vegetable Soufflé Pudding

> 1 package boil-in-a-bag creamed spinach
> 1 package boil-in-a-bag peas in onion sauce
> 1 package boil-in-a-bag Creole succotash
> 4 egg yolks, beaten
> 1 teaspoon salt
> ¼ teaspoon white pepper
> ½ cup grated Parmesan cheese
> 4 egg whites, beaten stiff

Heat all the vegetables by placing bags in boiling water; cook 10 minutes. Empty bags into a bowl; mix in the egg yolks, salt, pepper and cheese. Cool 10 minutes. Fold in the egg whites. Turn into a 1½-quart soufflé or baking dish. Bake in a preheated 375° oven 30 minutes, or until set. Serve immediately. Serves 6-8.

*   *   *

Corn was the staple food of the Indians of North and South America, a fact reported by the hordes of European explorers who came in hopes of finding gold or new routes to the Indies, or in search of new lands to conquer. Not only was the corn eaten on the cob by the Indians but several tribes knew how to grind it for flour, from which they made pancakes and primitive breads. The Indians of Mexico learned how to make a sweet, honey-like syrup from the stalks, the Incas turned the corn into sugar; but for some undiscovered reason, *every* tribe knew how to make a strong liquor from distilled corn.

It was undoubtedly Columbus who first brought corn to Europe. Only fifty years later, it had traveled around the world to the remotest corners of the Far East, a record for speed when considered in the light of the state of communications of the early 16th century.

*   *   *

"Comer verdura y echar mal ventura." Eat vegetables and be healthy.

Old Spanish Proverb, 18th century

Salads

Mixed Green Salad

Almost any combination of greens may be used in making the classic Mixed Green Salad. Use two different kinds of greens at least, preferably three or four. It is not necessary, however, to have more than that.

A combination might be made from several of the following: Simpson, Boston or Iceberg lettuce (only one from this group), romaine, escarole, chicory, endive, watercress. Bibb (Kentucky limestone) lettuce. Wash the greens very carefully, and see that they are crisp and cold. When ready to serve, wipe them dry with paper toweling, and then *tear* the leaves (do not cut them) into bite-sized pieces. Add French dressing just before serving and toss lightly until greens are well coated.

Tomatoes are not served with the classic Mixed Green Salad.

Asparagus Salad

> 2 pounds asparagus
> 1/4 cup vegetable oil
> 2 tablespoons soy sauce
> 1/2 teaspoon sugar
> 1/8 teaspoon Tabasco

Cut all the white part of the asparagus away. Cut the green part diagonally into 1-inch pieces. Cover with boiling water, then drain well immediately. Chill.

Mix together the oil, soy sauce, sugar and Tabasco. Toss with the asparagus just before serving. Serves 4-6.

Caesar Salad

> 3 heads romaine lettuce
> 1 cup olive oil
> 2 cups bread cubes
> 2 cloves garlic, minced
> 1 teaspoon salt
> ½ teaspoon dry mustard
> ½ teaspoon freshly ground black pepper
> 6 anchovies
> ¼ cup wine vinegar
> 1 egg, coddled 1 minute
> ¾ cup grated Parmesan cheese

Wash the lettuce carefully; drain well and chill. When ready to prepare the salad, dry the leaves thoroughly with paper toweling. Then *break* or *tear* the leaves by hand (do not cut them with a knife) into large pieces; place in a large bowl. Heat ½ cup oil in a skillet; add the bread cubes and garlic. Sauté until browned.

Sprinkle the lettuce with the salt, mustard, pepper, anchovies and remaining oil. Toss lightly with 2 spoons until well coated. Sprinkle with the vinegar and toss again. Break the egg into the salad, and toss until it is completely distributed. Add the cheese and toss again. Just before serving, toss in the croutons (browned bread cubes). Serves 6-8.

Mixed Bean Salad

> 1½ cups cooked or canned dried lima beans
> 1½ cups cooked or canned kidney beans
> 1 cup thinly sliced onions
> 1 cup chopped celery
> ¾ cup olive or vegetable oil
> ¼ cup wine vinegar
> 1 clove garlic, minced
> ¾ teaspoon salt
> ¼ teaspoon freshly ground black pepper
> 1 teaspoon chili powder

Toss together the lima beans, kidney beans, onions and celery. Beat together oil, vinegar, garlic, salt, pepper and chili powder. Pour over the bean mixture and chill 2 hours before serving. Serves 6-8.

Kidney Bean Salad

> 2 cans kidney beans
> ¼ cup wine vinegar
> ¼ cup lemon juice
> ¾ cup olive or salad oil
> 1 teaspoon salt
> ½ teaspoon freshly ground black pepper
> 1 clove garlic, minced
> ¼ cup chopped scallions (green onions)
> 3 tablespoons chopped parsley

Drain the beans very well. Beat together the vinegar, lemon juice, oil, salt, pepper and garlic. Toss the dressing with the beans, scallions and parsley. Marinate 3 hours in refrigerator. Serve on lettuce. Serves 6-8.

Cold Broccoli in Sour Cream

> 2 packages frozen broccoli
> 2 tablespoons cream cheese
> 1 tablespoon tomato paste
> ¾ teaspoon salt
> 1 cup sour cream
> 2 tablespoons chopped green olives

Cook the broccoli 1 minute less than package directs. Drain and chill. Mash the cheese; blend in the tomato paste and salt, then gradually stir in the sour cream. Fold in the olives. Spoon over the broccoli. Serves 4-6.

Cauliflower Salad

> 1 small cauliflower, or 1 package frozen
> ¾ cup julienne-cut green peppers

½ cup cooked or canned sliced beets
½ cup olive oil
3 tablespoons wine vinegar
1 teaspoon salt
¼ teaspoon freshly ground black pepper
2 tablespoons minced chives

Break the fresh cauliflower into flowerets. Cook the
fresh or frozen cauliflower in boiling salted water until
tender but crisp. Drain well and chill. Toss with the
green peppers and beets.

Beat together the oil, vinegar, salt, pepper and chives.
Pour over the vegetables. Chill 30 minutes before serving.
Serves 4-6.

Chiffonade Salad

3 hard-cooked eggs, chopped
3 tomatoes, peeled and quartered
2 tablespoons minced chives or scallions (green
    onions)
1 cup shredded romaine lettuce
1 cup shredded Simpson or Boston lettuce
1 cup shredded chicory or escarole
1 cup shredded water cress
1 cup chopped cooked or canned beets

Combine all of the above ingredients in a bowl and let
chill.
Prepare the following dressing:

½ cup tarragon vinegar
¾ cup olive oil
¾ teaspoon salt
¼ teaspoon freshly ground black pepper
2 teaspoons minced chives
2 teaspoons minced fresh chervil (or ⅛ teaspoon
    dried)
2 teaspoons minced capers
2 hard-cooked egg yolks, mashed
½ teaspoon dry mustard

Beat all of the above ingredients together until quite smooth. Pour over the salad, mix lightly and serve immediately. Serves 6-8.

Coleslaw with Apples

3 cups shredded cabbage
½ cup grated carrots
¾ cup thinly sliced apples
3 tablespoons chopped celery
½ cup mayonnaise
¼ cup sour cream
¾ teaspoon celery salt
⅛ teaspoon Tabasco

Toss together the cabbage, carrots, apples and celery. Mix until smooth the mayonnaise, sour cream, celery salt and Tabasco. Toss with the vegetables and serve. Serves 4-6.

Coleslaw with Buttermilk Dressing

6 cups shredded cabbage
¼ cup finely chopped onions
¼ cup grated carrots
¼ cup cider vinegar
3 tablespoons vegetable oil
1 teaspoon salt
¼ teaspoon white pepper
1 teaspoon sugar
½ cup buttermilk

Cover the shredded cabbage with ice water for 15 minutes. Drain well, then toss with the onions and carrots. Bring to a boil the vinegar, oil, salt, pepper and sugar. Pour over the cabbage and toss. Let stand 10 minutes, then mix in the buttermilk. Chill. Serves 6-8.

Coleslaw with Olives

> 4 cups shredded cabbage
> ½ cup thinly sliced scallions (green onions)
> ¼ cup chopped green pepper
> 1 cup sliced green pepper
> ½ cup mayonnaise
> 2 tablespoons heavy cream
> 2 teaspoons Worcestershire sauce
> ½ teaspoon salt
> ⅛ teaspoon freshly ground black pepper
> ½ teaspoon dried dill

Toss together the cabbage, scallions, green pepper and olives. Mix together the mayonnaise, cream, Worcestershire sauce, salt, pepper and dill. Chill cabbage mixture and dressing separately until 5 minutes before serving time, then toss together. Serves 6-8.

Cheese-Stuffed Lettuce

> 1 firm head of lettuce
> ¼ pound cream cheese
> 1 cup cottage cheese
> 2 tablespoons sour cream
> 2 tablespoons minced onion
> ¼ cup chopped green pepper
> ½ cup grated carrots
> ½ teaspoon salt
> ¼ teaspoon pepper
> ¼ cup chopped nuts

Wash the lettuce, drain and dry. Cut out the core, making a cavity large enough to hold cheese mixture.

Beat together the cream cheese, cottage cheese, sour cream and onion. Mix in the green pepper, carrots, salt, pepper and nuts. Stuff the lettuce; chill several hours. Cut into wedges and serve with French dressing. Serves 5-6.

Italian Onion Salad

>   4 large red Italian or sweet Spanish onions
>   2 teaspoons salt
>   ½ cup olive oil
>   3 tablespoons wine vinegar
>   8 anchovy fillets
>   ¼ cup pitted black olives (Italian or Greek)

Peel the onions and slice paper thin. Cover with ice water; add the salt and a few ice cubes. Let stand 30 minutes. Drain the onions and dry. Put the onions in a salad bowl; sprinkle with a mixture of the oil and vinegar. Arrange the anchovies and olives on top. Serves 6-8.

Mushroom Salad

>   1½ pounds mushrooms
>   ¾ cup olive oil
>   3 tablespoons lemon juice or white wine vinegar
>   1½ teaspoons salt
>   ¼ teaspoon freshly ground black pepper

Buy very fresh, firm white mushrooms. Remove the stems and use for another purpose. Peel the caps and slice paper-thin. Mix together the oil, lemon juice, salt and pepper. Toss with the mushrooms. Chill 2 hours before serving in lettuce cups. Serves 6-8.

Onion-Cucumber Salad

>   2 onions
>   2 cucumbers
>   ½ cup cider vinegar
>   ¼ cup water
>   1 teaspoon sugar
>   1 teaspoon salt
>   ¼ teaspoon freshly ground black pepper

Peel the onions and cucumbers; cut into paper-thin slices. Cover with salted ice water. Cover and chill for 3-4 hours. Drain; add the vinegar, water, sugar, salt and pepper. Serves 4-6.

Pepper Salad

> ⅓ cup cider vinegar
> 3 tablespoons vegetable oil
> 1 teaspoon salt
> ¼ teaspoon white pepper
> ½ teaspoon mustard seeds
> 1 teaspoon celery seeds
> 2 tablespoons brown sugar
> 4 cups chopped cabbage
> 4 peppers (green and red), chopped
> 2 tablespoons finely chopped onion

Mix together the vinegar, oil, salt, pepper, mustard seeds, celery seeds and brown sugar. Toss together the cabbage, peppers and onion. Add the dressing and mix thoroughly. Chill for 3 hours before serving. Serves 6-8.

Hot Potato Salad

> 2 pounds small potatoes
> ¼ pound bacon
> ½ cup chopped onion
> ⅓ cup cider vinegar
> ½ cup light cream
> 1 teaspoon salt
> ¼ teaspoon freshly ground black pepper

Cook the unpeeled potatoes until tender but firm. Slip off the skins immediately and slice the potatoes. Prepare the dressing while the potatoes are cooking.

Fry the bacon crisp, remove and crumble. Pour off half the fat. Sauté the onion in the fat 10 minutes. Stir in the vinegar, cream, salt, pepper and crumbled bacon. Bring to a boil and pour over the potatoes. Serves 6-8.

Salade Niçoise

>   1 large romaine lettuce
>   1 teaspoon salt
>   ½ teaspoon freshly ground black pepper
>   1 cucumber, sliced
>   2 tomatoes, cut into eighths
>   2 tablespoons capers
>   ¾ cup thinly sliced onions (red, if available)
>   1 7¾ ounce can tuna fish in chunks
>   1 green pepper, cut julienne
>   1 clove garlic, minced
>   ½ cup olive oil
>   3 tablespoons wine vinegar
>   ½ teaspoon dry mustard
>   3 hard-cooked eggs, quartered
>   ½ cup sliced black olives

Salade Niçoise, the famous appetizer salad of the French Riviera, is prepared in many different ways, of which this is merely one example. The tuna fish may be omitted, and replaced with sliced, cooked potatoes. This salad is always served as an appetizer, never with or after main courses. However, it is excellent as a hot-weather lunch.

Have the lettuce crisp and cold; dry it with paper towels and then tear it (do not cut) into bite-sized pieces in a large bowl. Add the salt, pepper, cucumber, tomatoes, capers, onions, tuna and green pepper. Mix lightly. Beat together the garlic, oil, vinegar and mustard. Pour over the salad and toss until well blended. Garnish with the eggs and olives. Serves 4.

Cucumber Dressing

>   1 cup finely chopped cucumbers
>   ½ teaspoon salt
>   1 tablespoon lemon juice
>   1 tablespoon minced dill (optional)
>   1 cup sour cream

Drain the cucumbers very well. Mix with the salt, lemon juice and dill. Fold into the sour cream. Chill. Serve with sea food or vegetable salads. Makes about 2 cups.

Parsley Dressing

> 3 tablespoons minced parsley
> ¼ cup finely chopped dill pickle
> ¼ cup chopped tomatoes
> ¼ teaspoon salt
> 1 cup sour cream

Mix together the parsley, dill pickle, tomatoes and salt. Fold into the sour cream. Chill. Serve with sea food. Makes about 2 cups.

* * *

The cucumber is a vegetable that did not originate in one particular place, being found in many parts of the world even in prehistoric times. The Bible contains a very early reference to it, when the Israelites were wandering in the desert for forty years; they bemoaned the lack of their favorite vegetable, the juicy, succulent cucumber. Who could blame them, wandering about in that hot desert?

There are Chinese writings dating back fifteen hundred years which contain specific references to the cucumber; the Romans had cucumbers, small and gnarled, but cucumbers nonetheless, for their elaborate salads. When European explorers came to the New World, they found cucumbers growing wherever they went.

Many of the skin imperfections, the knobs and prickles, the spines and warts, that originally detracted from the appearance of the cucumber, have been eliminated by selective horticulture. Most of the new varieties are quite straight, whereas the original was curved in the shape of a half-moon.

〜〜〜〜〜〜〜〜〜〜〜〜〜〜〜〜〜〜〜〜〜

Carrot Tea Bread

1½ cups sifted flour
½ teaspoon salt
1 teaspoon double-acting baking powder
¾ teaspoon baking soda
1 teaspoon cinnamon
1½ sticks (⅔ cup) butter
1 cup sugar
2 eggs
1 cup grated raw carrots
¼ cup chopped pecans or walnuts

Preheat oven to 350°. Grease a 12-inch loaf pan.
Sift together the flour, salt, baking powder, baking soda and cinnamon. Cream the butter and sugar until thick and fluffy. Add 1 egg at a time, beating well after each addition. Gradually stir in the flour mixture until smooth. Mix in the carrots and nuts. Turn into the prepared pan. Bake 1 hour, or until top springs back when pressed lightly with the finger. Invert and cool on a cake rack.

Carrot Torte

12 egg yolks
¾ cup sugar
½ cup grated carrots
¾ cup ground almonds
½ cup grated apple
1 teaspoon lemon juice
12 egg whites

Preheat the oven to 375°. Grease a 10-inch spring form and dust with flour.

Beat the egg yolks; add the sugar, beating until light and fluffy. Stir in the carrots, almonds, apple and lemon juice.

Beat the egg whites until stiff, but not dry; fold into the carrot mixture. Turn into the prepared pan. Bake 45 minutes, or until a cake tester comes out clean. Cool before removing from pan. Delicious with whipped cream. Serves 10-12.

Sweet Potato Biscuits

> 1 cup sifted flour
> ¾ teaspoon salt
> ¼ teaspoon nutmeg
> 2 teaspoons double-acting baking powder
> ⅓ cup shortening
> 1 cup mashed sweet potatoes
> ⅓ cup light cream

Sift together the flour, salt, nutmeg and baking powder. Cut in the shortening with a pastry blender or 2 knives. Work in the sweet potatoes and cream. On a lightly floured surface, knead the dough about 5 minutes. Roll out ½-inch thick. Cut with a floured biscuit cutter. Transfer to a greased baking sheet. For soft biscuits, place close together. For crisp ones, leave space between each. Bake in a preheated 450° oven 12 minutes, or until browned.

Makes about 24 biscuits.

Sweet Potato Cake

> 1½ cups sifted flour
> ½ teaspoon salt
> 2 teaspoons baking powder
> ¼ pound butter
> ¾ cup sugar
> 2 eggs

2 cups mashed sweet potatoes
1 teaspoon nutmeg
1 tablespoon lemon juice
½ cup milk

Sift together the flour, salt and baking powder. Cream the butter; beat in the sugar until light and fluffy. Add one egg at a time, beating after each addition. Beat in the potatoes, nutmeg and lemon juice. Add the flour mixture, alternately with the milk; blend well.

Turn into a greased 9-inch loaf pan. Bake in a preheated 325° oven 1 hour, or until a cake tester comes out clean. Cool on a cake rack. Ice with a lemon icing.

NOTE: This is a moist, not very sweet cake, more suitable as a tea bread than as a dessert.

Sweet Potato Custard Pudding

1½ sticks (⅔ cup) butter
1 cup packed brown sugar
½ teaspoon salt
2 eggs
2 cups grated raw sweet potatoes
2 tablespoons grated orange rind
½ teaspoon powdered ginger
½ teaspoon mace
2 tablespoons cognac

Cream the butter, gradually adding the sugar; add salt and beat until light and fluffy. Beat in 1 egg at a time, then the sweet potatoes, orange rind, ginger, mace and cognac. Turn into a buttered 8-by-12-inch baking dish. Bake in a preheated 350° oven 1 hour. Serve warm, cut into squares, with cognac-flavored whipped cream. Serves 4-6.

Sweet Potato Nut Pie

4 eggs
½ cup packed brown sugar
1½ cups mashed sweet potatoes

   ¼ teaspoon salt
   ⅔ cup light cream
   ⅓ cup orange juice
   ½ cup chopped walnuts or pecans
   1 teaspoon vanilla extract
   9-inch unbaked pastry shell

Beat the eggs and sugar until thick. Beat in the potatoes, then the salt, cream and orange juice. Stir in the nuts and vanilla. Turn into the lined pie plate.

Bake in a preheated 425° oven 10 minutes. Reduce heat to 375° and bake 30 minutes longer, or until firm. Cool. Serve with nutmeg-flavored whipped cream.

Sweet Potato-Pineapple Pudding

   3 cups mashed sweet potatoes
   2 tablespoons butter
   ⅓ cup honey
   ½ cup heavy cream
   ½ teaspoon salt
   ½ teaspoon powdered ginger
   2 egg yolks, beaten
   ½ cup drained, crushed, canned pineapple
   2 eggs whites, beaten stiff

Beat together the potatoes, butter, honey, cream, salt, and ginger. Beat in the egg yolks, then stir in the pineapple. Fold in the egg whites. Turn into a buttered baking dish. Bake in a preheated 325° oven 1 hour, or until browned and set. Serve warm, with whipped cream, if desired. Serves 4-6.

Sweet Potato Whip

   2 pounds sweet potatoes
   ½ cup hot light cream
   3 tablespoons butter
   ½ teaspoon salt

¼ teaspoon ginger
⅛ teaspoon nutmeg
3 tablespoons ground nuts

Cook the sweet potatoes until tender; peel and mash.
Beat in the cream, butter, salt, ginger and nutmeg until
very fluffy. Turn into a buttered 1½-quart casserole;
sprinkle with the nuts. Bake in a 400° oven 20 minutes,
or until browned. Serves 6-8.

Pumpkin Custard

2 eggs
½ cup packed brown sugar
½ teaspoon salt
¼ teaspoon nutmeg
¼ teaspoon powdered ginger
1 cup cooked puréed pumpkin
1 cup heavy cream
1 tablespoon cognac
2 tablespoons grated orange rind

Beat the eggs, sugar, salt, nutmeg and ginger until
blended. Mix in the pumpkin, then the cream, cognac
and orange rind. Pour into 6 buttered custard cups. Set
the cups in a shallow pan of hot water. Bake in a preheated 325° oven 40 minutes, or until a knife inserted
in the center comes out clean. Remove the cups from the
pan. Serve warm or cold, with ginger-flavored whipped
cream. Serves 6.

Pumpkin Custard Pie

1½ cups puréed pumpkin
3 egg yolks, beaten
1 cup packed brown sugar
½ teaspoon salt
½ teaspoon powdered ginger
½ teaspoon cinnamon

1½ cups sour cream
2 tablespoons grated orange rind
3 egg whites, stiffly beaten
9-inch pastry shell, baked 10 minutes and cooled

In a bowl, beat together the pumpkin, egg yolks, sugar, salt, ginger and cinnamon. Gradually mix in the sour cream. Pour into the top of a double boiler; place over hot water and cook, stirring steadily, until thickened. Cool 15 minutes, then fold in the orange rind and egg whites. Turn into the pie shell. Bake in a preheated 350° oven 25 minutes, or until set and browned. Serve warm or cold, with whipped cream flavored with orange liqueur.

Pumpkin Cream Pie

2 cups puréed pumpkin
⅔ cup brown sugar
½ teaspoon salt
1 teaspoon cinnamon
½ teaspoon powdered ginger
½ teaspoon nutmeg
1⅞ cups light cream
2 eggs, beaten
2 tablespoons cognac
9-inch unbaked pastry shell

Mix together the pumpkin, sugar, salt, cinnamon, ginger and nutmeg. Gradually beat in 1 cup cream until smooth. Beat the eggs, cognac and remaining cream. Beat into the pumpkin mixture. Turn into the pastry shell. Bake in a preheated 325° oven 50 minutes, or until a knife inserted in the center comes out clean. Serve warm.

Pumpkin Spice Cake

3 cups sifted flour
¼ teaspoon salt
2 teaspoons baking soda

        2 teaspoons cinnamon
        1 teaspoon ground allspice
        ¼ teaspoon powdered ginger
        ¼ pound butter
        ¾ cup packed brown sugar
        2 eggs
        2 cups puréed pumpkin

Sift together the flour, salt, baking soda, cinnamon, allspice and ginger. Cream the butter; gradually beat in the sugar until light and fluffy. Add 1 egg at a time, beating after each addition. Add the pumpkin alternately with the flour mixture, beating until well blended. Turn into a greased 12-inch loaf pan. Bake in a preheated 325° oven 40 minutes, or until a cake tester comes out clean. Cool on a cake rack.

Squash Pie

        3 egg yolks
        ½ cup sugar
        ⅛ cup melted butter
        1 teaspoon salt
        ½ teaspoon mace
        ½ teaspoon cinnamon
        1 teaspoon vanilla extract
        2 cups cooked puréed squash
        ¾ cup light cream
        3 egg whites, beaten stiff
        9-inch unbaked pastry shell

Beat the egg yolks and sugar until thick and light. Beat in the melted butter, salt, mace, cinnamon and vanilla. Mix together the squash and cream until smooth; beat into the yolk mixture, then fold in the egg whites.

Turn into the lined pie plate. Bake in a preheated 425° oven 10 minutes. Reduce heat to 375° and bake 20 minutes longer, or until firm. Cool.

Green Tomato Pie

Pastry for 2-crust pie
1 tablespoon melted butter
3 cups thinly sliced green tomatoes
½ cup brown sugar
5 tablespoons butter
3 cups thinly sliced apples
3 tablespoons apple brandy
2 tablespoons heavy cream

Line a 9-inch pie plate with half the pastry; brush with
the melted butter and chill 1 hour. Spread half the
tomatoes on the bottom. Sprinkle with some brown sugar
and dot with 1 tablespoon butter. Spread ½ the apples
over the tomatoes; sprinkle with brown sugar and dot
with butter. Cover with the remaining tomatoes; sprinkle
with sugar and dot with butter. Make second apple layer;
sprinkle with sugar and dot with butter. Pour the apple
brandy over all.

Roll out the remaining pastry, cover the pie and seal
the edges. Make a few slits in the top; brush with the
cream. Bake in a preheated 375° oven 40 minutes, or
until browned. Serve warm or cold.

Baked Yams and Coconut

4 medium yams (1½ pounds), or 1 1-pound can yams
½ cup flaked coconut
¼ cup seedless raisins
1 tablespoon grated lemon rind
½ teaspoon powdered ginger
¼ cup lemon juice
2 tablespoons melted butter

Cook the fresh yams until tender, but firm. Drain, peel
and cut in 1-inch slices. Or drain the canned yams; cut

n 1-inch slices. Arrange the yams in a greased shallow
baking dish.

Mix together the coconut, raisins, lemon rind and
ginger. Spread over the yams. Pour the lemon juice mixed
with the butter over all. Bake in a preheated 350° oven
25 minutes, or until browned. Serves 4-6.

* * *

Pumpkin is a word with a fascinating history. The
original Greek word for this vegetable actually means
mellow, or sun-ripened, as most pumpkins grow into full
maturity with plenty of sunshine. The original Greek
word was modified by the French into *pompion*, and sub-
sequently became "punkin"; ultimately it reached its
final form as "pumpkin."

In England, the word "pumpkin" is sometimes used
to mean a large squash. The English marrow, or vegetable marrow, however, is not a pumpkin, but a long,
narrow squash.

As if all of this were not confusing enough, the Algon-
quin Indian word "squash" actually means green or un-
ripe. Contrast this meaning with the Greek word for
pumpkin—mellow, or sun-ripened.

* * *

Sweet potatoes are generally believed to have origi-
nated in India, from which point they moved into Burma
and Thailand. These delicious tubers are very popular
throughout southeast Asia even today.

On the other hand, there are those who believe that
sweet potatoes were first grown on the American conti-
nents, North and South, and then brought to Europe.

* * *

"Now good digestion, wait on appetite, and health on
both."

Shakespeare: *Macbeth*

Index